A SPIRITUAL JOURNEY
into the WORLD WHERE GOD LIVES

How God reveals himself

Robert J. Morgart

xulon PRESS

Copyright © 2016 by Robert J. Morgart

A spiritual journey into the world where God lives
How God reveals himself
by Robert J. Morgart

Printed in the United States of America.

ISBN 9781498484701

All rights reserved solely by the author. The author guarantees all contents are original and do not infringe upon the legal rights of any other person or work. No part of this book may be reproduced in any form without the permission of the author. The views expressed in this book are not necessarily those of the publisher.

Unless otherwise indicated, Scripture quotations taken from the New Living Translation (NLT). Copyright © 1996, 2004, 2007 by Tyndale House Foundation. Used by permission. All rights reserved.

www.xulonpress.com

Foreword

*A*ny commentary in counseling is like a visual description of a mountain or island: It is never completed or exhausted, just because it's given from a definite point of view. Dr. Morgart's expositions are offered from a point of view, and his viewing points are systematic and practical. His flow of thought gives the reader both clarity and classic study for comparisons.

Daniel 2:22 says: "He reveals the deep and secret things; he knows what is in the darkness and the light dwells with Him" (NIV). Dr. Morgart encourages those penetrating the dark areas of the heart, as well as areas of hurt that require freedom. The author assures us that Jesus Christ will be with us all the way. The promise is: "Being confident of this very thing, that He who has begun a good work in you will complete it until the day of Jesus Christ" (Phil. 1:6).

These words become a testimony to him as we share with others his cleansing and restoration. Yes, Dr. Morgart shows in this volume the possibility and probability of freedom from bondage with Jesus as

A spiritual journey into the world where God lives

Lord of our lives. The reality of life, hope, and purpose surpasses all understanding.

Dr. Dwight Martin

Florida Beacon College & Seminary
P.O. Box 8135
Jacksonville, FL 32239-8135

ACKNOWLEDGMENTS

First and foremost, I acknowledge the Holy Spirit who kept me up many nights writing thoughts in my notebook and bringing Scripture references to light.

To all the writers of the Bible who were inspired to author the divine declaration of God's Grace to Mankind.

To my wife Susan, who supported and assisted me over the many months it has taken to produce my first book.

To my friend Dr. Dwight Martin, who encouraged me to write this book.

To my mother-in-law Alma, for her patience and support.

To my colleges and servants of the Lord, who have given me precious spiritual insight, prophesied and prayed for me and my family, and encouraged me to write this book.

To the angelic hosts who have who have ministered to us and protected us from the throws of the evil one.

A spiritual journey into the world where God lives

To the many Christian writers, books, and materials that have contributed to my spiritual knowledge and understanding, and inspired many topics in this book.

For the many Christians who have added their knowledge to my own while reading and editing sections of this book.

AUTHOR

After walking with God for most of my life, it has become quite evident that God has a great deal to say to us and to impress upon us concerning our spiritual lives. It is stressed many times in the New Testament that we are to walk with Jesus in this life and into the next.

By allowing ourselves to be divinely guided by His Holy Spirit, we awaken to the life God intended for us. He is our counselor, our guide, and our life's director. It is because of God's Holy Word and His Spirit within us that we are able to see, in part, through His eyes.

> Psalms 32:8—I will instruct you and teach you in the way you should go; I will counsel you with my eye upon you.

As a young Christian, my search for spiritual meaning kept me probing God's Word for satisfying and complete answers. One of the problems I encountered was when I was aspiring to seek spiritual meaning through God's Word, I often ended up just seeking after my own interests. Although I tried to make His thoughts, my thoughts and His ways my ways, I still found it hard to tell the difference between what was God and what was just me. I often found that "I" seemed to be much easier to find; wherever I looked for God, there I was, ready for all the attention. In times of trouble, I expected God to immediately come galloping in on a white horse and rescue me. When this did not happen, I would lose faith. It was apparent that I wanted to have total control over my life rather than letting the Lord of all creation guide and direct my earthly journey.

It was not until later in my Christian life that I felt the awesome presence of God and began seeing into His world. God kept me on His molding wheel shaping me over and over again until I clearly understood that a life without Him is no life at all. I fell off the Potter's wheel more than once where God had to pick me up and start all over again. He showed me that sometimes suffering great pain was necessary to learn compassion for others and to understand more fully His grace.

I have always had a persistent desire to understand my relationship with God and His relationship with me. I knew to live a godly life I was to set my sights on heaven, not this world, and walk in the Spirit of God. Okay, but what does all that really mean? How do we not live in this world and live as if we were already living with our heavenly Father? Do we not need to know what God requires of us and to know what we are setting our sights on? I heard for years that a Christian's goal was this place called Heaven where his treasures are stored, but no one could tell me what Heaven would be like or what my treasures would be. So I began a quest to find answers.

Although I still have many questions about heaven and our rightful place in it, I would like to share with you the results of my quest up to this point in my life. Please be aware that I see my journey as an ongoing and ever-changing quest. Each new spiritual challenge brings me closer to God. With increased knowledge, comes increased awareness and more questions.

INTRODUCTION

There are entire books on the market today, giving a Christian perspective on how God has communicated with His children throughout Church history. It is not the purpose of this book to talk about this history, but to investigate the question, "does God still communicate directly with His children today and if so, how?"

Throughout this book, we will be exploring who is this being we call God, what does the Bible tells us about heaven, and investigating other material that confirms or expands on these biblical narratives. The material we will look at, outside of the Bible, is not in any way meant to contradict the Bible, to be seen as equal to the Bible, or to supersede the Bible. I will also be sharing with you a variety of materials that will give you an idea of what heaven, or hell may be like once you get there.

When we talk about heaven, coming home at the end of our earthly journey offers us the greatest and highest rewards, but the path along the way can be an awesome adventure. As you walk along your spiritual journey, you must be lighthearted and adventurous; open to God's revelations as you get to know Him and learn more about where He lives. It is reasonable to believe that along your journey you will experience a strong sense of His presence and learn to connect with Him in ways you have never experienced before.

We will explore together what it means to see into God's world. With the Spirit of God as our inspiration, guide and teacher, we can expand our knowledge and understanding of the world where God lives.

There are topics discussed in this book that may seem controversial and seen in a different light than you are used to. God speaks to us in many different ways, and it is okay for us to have different interpretations in areas of the Bible that are open to personal question. Many respected theologians often differ in their opinions when it comes to questionable biblical doctrine. Look at all the theological differences in the many Christian denominations. Where believers do not differ is in the fundamental doctrines of who God is, who Jesus is, and why God sent His Son to die for us. These core doctrines and other topics will be covered throughout this book. It is not the intent of this book that you see things the way I see them, but to allow you to see into a world of eloquent grace and eternal beauty.

Know always, as spiritual beings, we are intimately loved and supported by our Creator. We are given the power to rise above earthly ways and live a life according to God's spiritual laws. The way is not difficult, stop being resistant and start listening to the loving support your spirit has to offer. God is waiting and delighted to help.

> 2 Corinthians 4:18—So we don't look at the troubles we can see now; rather, we fix our gaze on things that cannot be seen. For the things we see now will soon be gone, but the things we cannot see will last forever.

-So Many Questions—Too Few Answers-

Early in my Christian life I had many questions about God and His rightful place in it. If God is pure and only good comes from Him, where does evil come from? I reasoned that if God, and God alone, was the creator of all there is, then evil must have been inherent in His nature from the beginning. If this is true, then God could not be all good.

What happens to all those people who have never had an occasion to hear about God? Are they condemned to hell for their lack of knowledge? The Bible seemed to me at first to imply this. What about good people who have found a sense of purpose and happiness in their lives; why do they need God?

What about people who have heard about God and seem to have a pure heart (a good person) yet do not accept Him? Do they go to hell in spite of being good? If this is true, then you could question God's fairness. What about people of other faiths that dedicate their lives to moral living, kindness towards others, and respect for the earth and all its creatures? Is their penalty hellfire or no afterlife? It just did not seem reasonable that an all-loving God would keep all these people out of His eternal kingdom.

My logic dictated that an all-loving and merciful God would forgive all people of their sins and allow them into heaven. However, I seemed to be wrong; I was told that this is not what the Bible teaches. Scripture is quite clear that humanity is under the curse of sin, and if our sins are not forgiven, eternal separation from God (or possibly hell) is the result. So how do we reconcile a loving and merciful God with sin and hell?

These questions plagued my early Christian life and caused me to seriously question just who God is. I knew that somewhere there had to be simple logical answers to my questions.

In my search for answers, I realized that Christians and Theologians alike were perplexed by these questions. Over the years, from my biblical studies and the writings of many creditable Christians and Theologians, I have come to a point in my spiritual life where I believe I have found satisfactory answers to at least some of these questions.

The pages of this book testify to the fact that a divine God has the ability to interact in our lives and that the spiritual world, where He lives can be known.

It is important to note here that our next life is a testament of how we have lived our earthly life. In my study of the biblical heavens, ancient religious manuscripts, near-death experiences, and my own out-of-body visions,

Introduction

I have come to understand that there is not just one great big heaven, but heaven consists of many dwelling places.

> John 14:2—There is more than enough room in my Father's home (Dwelling Places, Realms, Mansions). If this were not so, would I have told you that I am going to prepare a place for you?

-The Never Ending Story-

I have always liked a good mystery, where the author draws you into the story and makes you a part of the plot. The author gives you little hints to the ending of the story but leaves you wanting. The anticipation of the mystery builds as you follow the storyline. You begin to ask yourself questions: What will the final outcome be? Is the protagonist (good guy) going to overcome the antagonist (bad guy)? You find some of your questions being answered as the plot thickens and draws you deeper into the story.

As you have more and more glorious adventures, the anticipation and excitement rises as you get closer to the end of the story. You feel that you will finally have the answers you are so desperately seeking. You cannot wait for the story to end, but as the story mystery unfolds, you find that the greatest thing about the story is that it just keeps getting better and better. You finally realize that the story brings such joy to you that you never really want it to end.

A spiritual journey into the world where God lives

This book contains some of the answers I have found along my journey in the never ending story. Although your answers may not be the same as mine, it is my fervent prayer that you will find your personal story as rewarding and fulfilling as my own.

> Ephesians 3:9–11—I (Paul) was chosen to explain to everyone this mysterious plan that God, the Creator of all things, had kept secret from the beginning. God's purpose in all this was to use the church to display his wisdom in its rich variety to all the unseen rulers and authorities in the heavenly places. This was his eternal plan, which he carried out through Christ Jesus our Lord.

-Analyzing Scripture-

Let me start by saying the Bible is the inerrant Word of God. However, interpreting the Bible correctly is another matter. When I need to interpret a difficult passage of Scripture, I pray, then I look at the context in which it was written, to whom it was written, the time period in which it was written, what was it meant to convey, answer, or explain, and if there is any other scripture that supports it. At this point, if I feel comfortable with the interpretation, I look at how it relates to human history and what, if any, empirical evidence(evidence being proved or disproved by observation) brings light to its understanding.

Introduction

After "studying to be approved," am I sure that I have the absolute answer? No! I have found there are many occasions when God brings new insight to scripture that I have missed. I would like to say that I have the absolute answers, but I do not. What I will say is "the Gospel of Jesus Christ needs no interpretation" and "God is the final answer."

It is my belief there is no greater truth than the Word of God and that many scriptures and biblical narratives speak to us in a way that requires no explanation. I have included many of these verses and narratives throughout this book. If any of these verses or narratives speaks to your heart, please take devotional time to meditate on them before continuing on.

> Joshua 1:8—Study this Book of Instruction (God's Holy Word) continually. Meditate on it day and night so you will be sure to obey everything written in it. Only then will you prosper and succeed in all you do.

When answering biblical questions, I use the words of the Holy Spirit inspired text, because God's words are mightier and speak louder than my own words ever could. Let God's Word speak to you. All scripture in this book is from the New Living Translation Bible (NLT) unless noted otherwise. I believe the English New Living Translation brings new light and understanding to God's Word. Emphasis added to scripture is in quotes.

A spiritual journey into the world where God lives

-The Immaterial Parts of Man-

According to the Bible, Man is distinct from the rest of creation in that he was made in the image of God. As God is tripartite—Father, Son, and Holy Spirit—so Man has three parts—spirit, soul and body.

The Apostle Paul writes to the church in Thessalonia:

> 1 Thessalonians 5:23—Now may the God of peace make you holy in every way, and may your whole spirit and soul and body be kept blameless until our Lord Jesus Christ comes again.

Man is tethered to a physical body that can be seen and touched, but he is also made up of immaterial parts, which are intangible. These parts include, but not limited to, spirit, soul, intellect, will, emotions, mind, and conscience. These immaterial characteristics exist beyond the physical lifespan of the human body and are therefore eternal.

The Bible makes it clear that the soul and spirit are the primary immaterial parts of a human being, while the body is the physical container that tethers them to this world.

I am going to define the intangible parts of Man in the way I have come to understand them.

Introduction

Spirit—The Ethereal Embodiment of Your Soul

I like the word spirit because it is an elusive term, and no one seems to know exactly what it refers to. Some people conjure up widely differing ideas and beliefs about what it could mean. For this book, I define the human spirit as an animated life force given to you by God. Your spirit contains your soul—all the things that make you, you. It is your spirit (spiritual self) that when redeemed, interfaces with the Spirit of God.

> 1 Peter 3:18—Christ suffered for our sins once for all time. He never sinned, but he died for sinners to bring you safely home to God. He suffered physical death, but he was raised to life in the Spirit.

> 1 Peter 4:6—That is why the Good News was preached to those who are now dead— so although they were destined to die like all people, they now live forever with God in the Spirit.

> 1 Corinthians 15:45—The Scriptures tell us, "The first man, Adam, became a living person." But the last Adam—that is, Christ—is a life-giving Spirit.

Soul—The Essence of All That Makes You, You

Your soul is the storehouse of all that makes you, you. It sits between the spirit and the body; it contains the heart, mind, intellect, conscience, will, and personality. Your soul travels with your spirit when you die. While earthbound, your soul has one foot in the flesh and one foot in the spirit.

> Matthew 16:26—And what do you benefit if you gain the whole world but lose your own soul? Is anything worth more than your soul?

Heart—The Seat of Feelings and Emotions

Your heart is the center of your soul. Heart in spiritual terms, refers to both the inward and outward expressions of moral conduct, feelings, and emotions. Emotions come from your soul and are expressed as feelings in your consciousness.

> Jeremiah 17:10—But I, the Lord, search all hearts and examine secret motives. I give all people their due rewards, according to what their actions deserve."

Introduction

Mind—The Seat of Intellect and Reason

Mind refers to Man's intellect and reason expressed through thought, perception, memory, will, and imagination.

> Romans 12:2—Don't copy the behavior and customs of this world, but let God transform you into a new person by changing the way you think. Then you will learn to know God's will for you, which is good and pleasing and perfect.
>
> Ephesians 4:21–24—Since you have heard about Jesus and have learned the truth that comes from him, throw off your old sinful nature and your former way of life, which is corrupted by lust and deception. Instead, let the Spirit renew your thoughts and attitudes. Put on your new nature, created to be like God—truly righteous and holy.

Personality—Distinguishing Traits

Personality is the combination of all attributes (behavioral, emotional and mental states) that you express outwardly as a unique individual. Your spiritual self and your sinful self present themselves through your personality. Your spiritual self is the part of you that knows and follows God's moral laws. Your sinful self is the part of you that denies, or rationalizes away the moral laws God wrote on your heart. Your spiritual self and your sinful self will be discussed in more detail later.

Conscience—God's Divine Whisper

Conscience is a judgment of reason that tells us to do the morally right thing. It is the ability that allows us to distinguish between right or wrong actions. God tells us that we have an innate knowledge of His immutable (unchanging) laws written on our heart. For the conscience to maintain its reliability, it must be guided by our spiritual self or it can be seared to a point where it no longer allows us to differentiate between what is right and what is wrong.

> Isaiah 30:21—Your own ears will hear him. Right behind you a voice will say, "This is the way you should go," whether to the right or to the left.

> Romans 2:15—They demonstrate that God's law is written in their hearts, for their own conscience and thoughts either accuse them or tell them they are doing right.

> 1 Timothy 4:1–2—Now the Holy Spirit tells us clearly that in the last times some will turn away from the true faith; they will follow deceptive spirits and teachings that come

> from demons. These people are hypocrites and liars, and their consciences are dead.

Flesh (Sin in the body)—Revolves around the Self-Serving "I"

The word flesh in the Bible is most often used to represent the human body. But it is also used to represent the sin born within us (our sin nature). The sinful flesh acts around the idea that everything was created for our own entertainment and pleasure. It is an egocentric (self centered) deceptive nature that empowers the self-centered "I"—I need, I want.

The most devastating of all the manifestations of sin in the flesh are seen as the seven deadly sins. These are the sins that are believed to cause you to lose your soul. These sins of the flesh are an ancient classification of the most evil transgressions. They consist of lust, gluttony, greed, sloth, wrath, envy, and pride.

> Romans 8:3—The Law of Moses was unable to save us because of the weakness of our sinful nature. So God did what the law could not do. He sent his own Son in a body like the bodies we sinners have. And in that body God declared an end to sin's control over us by giving his Son as a sacrifice for our sins.

TABLE OF CONTENTS

Foreword v
Acknowledgments vii
Author.................................. ix
Introduction xiii
   -So Many Questions—Too Few Answers
   -The Never Ending Story
   -The Immaterial Parts of Man
1. God Unveiled...........................29
2. The Spirit of God......................57
3. Are You Listening?.....................84
4. Our Spiritual Senses 110
5. A Spiritual Awakening 134
6. Cultivating Spiritual Fruit...........160
7. A Leap of Faith.......................189
8. Is Heaven a Real Place? 214
9. Supernatural Dreams and Visions..... 258
10. Dreams and Visions, God's Lost
    Communication 284
11. Caught up to Heaven..................315
Closing Thoughts.........................353
Bibliography 357

Chapter One

God Unveiled

Psalm 46:10
"Be still and know that I am God."

Romans 1:20
For ever since the world was created, people
have seen the earth and sky. Through
everything God made, they can clearly see
his invisible qualities—his eternal power
and divine nature. So they have no excuse
for not knowing God.

In The Beginning

In the beginning, God created the heavens and the earth. This was not just the earth and what we see when we look out into the expanse of the night sky. All the stars, planets and galaxies that can be seen, only make up four percent of our universe. Scientists theorize that the other 96 percent is made of dark energy and dark matter—things that cannot be perceived, yet exist. God created the heavens and the earth—multiple realms or dimensions of existence. "The Heavenly Realms" in the Bible refers to spiritual realms that exists in parallel with our physical world. We can only see in three dimensions of physical space, so we assume what is in this space is all that exists. The spiritual world contains many realms of reality beyond what we can see and are just as real as the physical space we live in.

> Ephesians 2:6—For he raised us from the dead along with Christ and seated us with him in the heavenly realms because we are united with Christ Jesus.
>
> Colossians 1:16—For through him God created everything in the heavenly realms and on earth. He made the things we can see and the things we can't see—such as thrones, kingdoms, rulers, and authorities in the unseen world. Everything was created through him and for him.
>
> Luke 17:21—You won't be able to say, 'Here it is!' or 'It's over there!' For the Kingdom of God is already among you (in and around you)."

A Spiritual Journey

There are times when God opens our spiritual eyes to experience Him in a more profound way. This is called "Seeing through Spiritual Eyes."

Developing the ability to sense in the spiritual world comes naturally to some people. For others, it takes some practice, but we are all able to experience it as it is an inherent part of our spiritual connection to God. Our five spiritual senses bring us more in tune with our intuition, discerning the things of God. As God's children, it is time to reclaim our spiritual senses.

We are losing out on God's spiritual provision and prosperity today because we do not know about the spiritual world. In fact, when told about it many consider it nothing but fantasy.

> 1 John 1:1–2—We proclaim to you (Jesus) the one who existed from the beginning, whom we have heard and seen. We saw him with our own eyes and touched him with our own hands. He is the Word of life. This one who is life itself was revealed to us, and we have seen him. And now we testify and proclaim to you that he is the one who is eternal life. He was with the Father, and then he was revealed to us.

From the very beginning of creation, Man was given the unique privilege of direct communication with God.

Man was made in the image of God, and unique from other creatures.

> Genesis 2:7—Then the Lord God formed the man from the dust of the ground. He breathed the breath of life into the man's nostrils, and the man became a living person.

> Genesis 1:27—So God created human beings in his own image. In the image of God he created them; male and female he created them.

God created Man with a physical body that would be tethered to a physical world. He then breathed into the man (Adam), creating a living spirit with a soul. The measure of a Man comes from his spirit and his soul. When the body dies, the soul and the spirit live on.

When we open our heart and allow God's Spirit to come alive in us, we come into a holy union with our Creator. This union moves us to know our Creator in a more intimate and profound way. As we draw near to God, He opens us to His purpose and presence.

> Hebrews 7:19—For the law never made anything perfect. But now we have confidence in a better hope, through which we draw near to God.

> James 4:8—Come close to God, and God will come close to you. Wash your hands, you

sinners; purify your hearts, for your loyalty is divided between God and the world.

Spiritual Vision

As powerful as our eyes are they have one serious limitation, our eyes only see physical reality. When it comes to perceiving the reality of the spiritual world, our eyes are limited. But know that the spiritual world is just as real as the physical world. Never make the mistake of thinking the spiritual world is less accessible than the physical world. It is just as real and available to anyone who seeks it.

Everyone is capable of attaining spiritual sight. God gave this ability to all His children. Sadly, those who are unaware of this ability or those who choose to ignore it are spiritually blind.

> 2 Corinthians 4:3–4—If the Good News we preach is hidden behind a veil, it is hidden only from people who are perishing. Satan, who is the god of this world, has blinded the minds of those who don't believe. They are unable to see the glorious light of the Good News. They don't understand this message about the glory of Christ, who is the exact likeness of God.

It is the power of God's Spirit that gives us insight into His world. Seeing with spiritual eyes should be a part of our everyday experience. Our spiritual eyes are open when our spirit is lifted (spiritual energy level) to that of the spiritual world. God's Word is very clear that we have been given the ability to see into and hear from His world.

> 1 Corinthians 2:9-10—That is what the Scriptures mean when they say, "No eye has seen, no ear has heard, and no mind has imagined what God has prepared for those who love him." But it was to us that God revealed these things by his Spirit. For his Spirit searches out everything and shows us God's deep secrets.

> John 3:3—Jesus replied, "I tell you the truth, unless you are born again, you cannot see the Kingdom of God."

> Deuteronomy 4:29—But from there you will search again for the LORD your God. And if you search for him with all your heart and soul, you will find him.

Heaven—Outside the Realm of Science

I have always had a problem accepting that something invisible really exists. The statement, "do not question it, just accept it on faith" has never been one of my finer points. I have always thought faith should be backed up with facts, at least some. The more I researched and studied, looking for facts that would give me an understanding of this invisible world, the more real and visible it became.

> Matthew 7:7–8—Keep on asking, and you will receive what you ask for. Keep on seeking, and you will find. Keep on knocking, and the door will be opened to you. For everyone who asks, receives. Everyone who seeks, finds. And to everyone who knocks, the door will be opened.

Many scientists have long dismissed the truth of the spiritual world as being a fantasy; holding on to a physical world where they think all the answers exist. While scientific thinking has been proven extremely useful since it started, over two thousand years ago, it only serves the physical world. It deals with knowledge based on the operation of physical laws that tell us how things work in a physical world. Physical reality does not incorporate a spiritual world or for that matter, what it has to offer.

Scientists argue that everything that exists in our physical world must be proven according to the scientific method, which are a set of rules defining a three-dimensional material world. Yet, science lacks the ability to adequately explain non-material things; such as why the universe exists, what are emotions or feelings, what is consciousness, what is creativity, where do morals come from, why something is seen as beautiful, or why do living things exist at all? Most scientists would agree that there is knowledge and understanding far outside the realm of the physical world.

Christians argue that there are unseen worlds, ranging from the most abominable hell all the way to the most glorious kingdom where God lives. What if both arguments are right? What if our physical world is not the only world? Within our physical world the laws of science apply, however, would it not be possible that the laws of a spiritual world would be quite different?

Consider for a moment that these worlds could be seen and known to those who are willing to open their spiritual eyes and to seek the truth that comes from a spiritual world. Those who have experienced this spiritual transcendence are sure of this other reality and can testify to its existence.

Heaven and Science Coming Together

The Bible tells us that heaven contains indescribable places of incredible beauty, yet this spiritual world remains unknown to science. Heaven just does not fit anywhere in scientific thought. Without evidence of its existence within the physical world, it has been generally ignored by scientists, atheists, and humanists.

There are scientists who believe in God and heaven, but mainstream science leaves out what physics or mathematics cannot prove. There is a worldwide abundance of credible afterlife empirical evidence for dimensions beyond our own, but scientists have for the most part been ignoring it until recently. The discovery of a new scientific theory has brought evidence for the possible existence of other worlds, dimensions and an afterlife into present day physics.

Today, because of a new scientific theory called "Quantum Mechanics" (QM), there are now many in the scientific community beginning to recognize the possibility of being able to prove the existence of dimensions beyond our own that do not have to be based on our current classical physical laws.

This new scientific discovery no longer limits science to the atheistic or humanistic views of a self-centered universe. For centuries, misguided doctrines and philosophies have been the primary obstacles to the growth of both science and religion. In today's world, I see science and religion moving towards a more common future.

QM, states that subatomic units (quanta) are the building blocks of everything in our physical world. These subatomic units behave in some respects like particles (matter) and in other respects like waves (energy). QM also tells us that other dimensions of reality may exist within the same space as our universe and are based on the various energy levels that support them. The reason we cannot see these multi-dimensional energy levels is the same reason we cannot see radio or television waves; they exist beyond the frequency (vibrations) of three-dimensional sight.

These new QM principles have been proven by physicists mathematically and experimentally. I find the implications of this intriguing when it comes to having scientific evidence that helps to support the possibility of unseen worlds beyond our own. QM is a game changer when it comes to what determines the fabric of space and time, the nature of reality, and what consciousness is. We are going to look at some basic QM principles.

1. What we understand as matter, does not attain a fixed reality until it is observed by our conscious mind. When matter is observed it becomes particles and can then be seen. When matter is not observed it is energy waves. One of the most utilized scientific experiments to prove this is called the Double-Slit Experiment. It appears as though our minds determine reality by creating form at the instant we observe it. This implies that if we are not looking at something it does not exist as a material form. I do not know if our minds truly create reality, but I find it intriguing that our consciousness can affect the nature of matter.
Approximately 96% of the universe is not visible to us. Physicists believe the universe consists mostly of what has become known today as dark matter and dark energy, matter and energy that is invisible to us. Dark matter and dark energy are all around us. Could this unseen matter and energy account for the dimensions that are not visible to us?
2. Information can be transferred between two synchronized subatomic particles no matter what

the distance is between them. This explains why many people know instantly when something happens to someone they care for, even if that person is a great distance away. This tells us that space and time at the subatomic level may not be objectively real. Atoms are almost entirely empty space, and there appears to be nothing in between them. The nucleus (center of the atom) is again almost entirely empty space with what looks like the tiniest of particles rotating around. It seems likely that the smallest units of the universe are nothing more than whirling waves of energy. If this is true, which it seems to be, then everything is made up of energy waves and only takes on a physical form when it is observed. Observation causes these waves of energy to take on the form of various matter particles. This leads to the theory that our conscious minds form matter particles out of energy waves.

3. To explain the discrete form of everything you see, again takes us to the subatomic quantum level. It is believed that around everything there exists a quantum energy field responsible for giving subatomic units their structure and form. Things seem solid only because there is a quantum energy field (referred to as the Higgs field—theorized by Peter Ware Higgs, British physicist) that holds them together, so when things come into contact with one another, their energy fields collide. This energy field is seen as the glue that holds

everything in our universe together. Without this field holding the energy units together, nothing as we know it could exist. In the book of Corinthians, it tells us that "Jesus created all things, and by him all things are held together."

> Colossians 1:16–17—For through him God created everything in the heavenly realms and on earth. He made the things we can see and the things we can't see—such as thrones, kingdoms, rulers, and authorities in the unseen world. Everything was created through him and for him. He existed before anything else, and he holds all creation together.

Physicists today believe space and time are so intertwined that they cannot be separated, so they are often just referred as space-time. QM tells us that space and time (space-time) are just an illusion, not objectively real. If you are familiar with dream study or the study of near-death experiences you will understand that space and time, whether in a dream or in a heavenly excursion are not the same as when we are awake and conscious of the world we see around us.

If the theory of QM is true, then it seems possible consciousness creates various levels of reality. Since God is a fully conscious being, and His Spirit exists everywhere, would it not be possible His Spirit (the consciousness of God) is with us every moment of every day watching over us?

Psalms 139:16—You saw me before I was born. Every day of my life was recorded in your book. Every moment was laid out before a single day had passed.

C. S. Lewis—Christianity, if false, is of no importance, and if true, of infinite importance. The only thing it cannot be is moderately important.

In my study of hundreds of near-death and deathbed experiences, QM helps to explain why near-death experiencers encounter other realms of existence where physical laws as we know them do not apply.

God Created Us to Know Him

We can know the one true and living God through His written Word, the Bible, and the power of His Holy Spirit working in us. It is through His Word and the power of His Spirit that we come to understand the righteousness of God and all that He requires of us.

- Man is sinful and spiritually separated from God.

  Romans 6:23—For the wages of sin is death, but the free gift of God is eternal life through Christ Jesus our Lord.

- Jesus Christ is God's only provision for Man's redemption from sin.

  John 14:6—Jesus told him, "I am the way, the truth, and the life. No one can come to the Father except through me.

  1 Corinthians 15:3–6—I passed on to you what was most important and what had also been passed on to me. Christ died for our sins, just as the Scriptures said. He was buried, and he was raised from the dead on the third day, just as the Scriptures said. He was seen by Peter and then by the Twelve. Later, he was seen by more than 500 of his followers.

- We can know God as our personal friend.

  Revelation 3:20—Look! I stand at the door and knock. If you hear my voice and open the door, I will come in, and we will share a meal together as friends.

Theophany

The Manifestation of a Deity in a Form the Human Senses can perceive
(World English Dictionary)

A Theophany is a perceptible manifestation of God that can be perceived by the human senses. God appeared in the Old Testament period in several non-human forms. God appears to us in the New Testament in the human form of Jesus Christ.

> Colossians 1:15—Christ is the visible image of the invisible God. He existed before anything was created and is supreme over all creation,

> Deuteronomy 31:14–15—Then the Lord said to Moses, "The time has come for you to die. Call Joshua and present yourselves at the Tabernacle, so that I may commission him there." So Moses and Joshua went and presented themselves at the Tabernacle. And the Lord appeared to them in a pillar of cloud that stood at the entrance to the sacred tent.

> Exodus 13:21—The Lord went ahead of them. He guided them during the day with a pillar of cloud, and he provided light at night with

a pillar of fire. This allowed them to travel by day or by night.

The Bible makes it clear that God came to earth as a human, the incarnation of Jesus, a Theophany, but He has never been seen in His true form. According to God's Word, a vision of His glory would overwhelm the physical senses of any Man. A Man in his physical state would not be able to live in God's true presence.

> John 1:18—No one has ever seen God. But the unique One, who is himself God, is near to the Father's heart. He has revealed God to us.

> Exodus 33:20—But you may not look directly at my face, for no one may see me and live.

> 1 Timothy 6:16—He alone can never die, and he lives in light so brilliant that no human can approach him. No human eye has ever seen him, nor ever will. All honor and power to him forever! Amen.

Wonders of the Universe

Albert Einstein did not claim to be a Christian, but when he looked out at the wonders of the universe, he saw God there. When asked if he was an atheist, he said no.

I'm not an atheist. The problem involved is too vast for our limited minds. We are in the position of a little child entering a huge library filled with books in many languages. The child knows someone must have written those books. It does not know how. It does not understand the languages in which they are written. The child dimly suspects a mysterious order in the arrangement of the books but doesn't know what it is. That, it seems to me, is the attitude of even the most intelligent human being toward God. We see the universe marvelously arranged and obeying certain laws but only dimly understand these laws.

Retrieved 3/17/13 from rayfowler.org/sermons/gods-good-creation-series/knowing-god-through-his-creation

Accepting That There is a God

Would we not just love for someone to show us absolute evidence that God does exist? No arm-twisting, no statements like, "You just have to believe to know Him." Well, to experience God we first must accept that there is a God. If a person opposes even the possibility of there being a God, then any evidence can be rationalized and explained away.

When it comes to God's existence, the Bible says there are people who have seen sufficient evidence, but have overridden their conscience and allowed all evidence to be blocked by deception and lies. Paul in his letter to the Hebrews writes:

> Hebrews 11:6—And it is impossible to please God without faith. Anyone who wants to come to him must believe that God exists and that he rewards those who sincerely seek him.

So if the Bible so plainly teaches that getting to know God begins by simply accepting His existence by faith, why is it so difficult for so many people? Many have come to believe that Man is the master of his own destiny and has no need for God to rule over his fate—Man alone has all the qualities necessary to be his own god. This belief is commonly held by atheists, humanists, and some Christian cults. This is one of Satan's greatest deceptions. God reveals Himself to us in many ways, but if we close our eyes to His existence, then He will not be found.

When Peter made his great confession that Jesus was the Son of God, Jesus answered, "Flesh and blood hath not revealed it unto thee, but my Father which is in heaven" (Matthew 16:16–17). God revealed this revelation to Peter because of his strong belief that Jesus was God's Son, the true Messiah. We must ask God to ingrain this great truth in us. We must have an intense desire for the truth of God's Word and allow it to enlighten our minds and guide us in absolute truth (John 14:26; 16:13).

We must go to the Bible ourselves, read it, study it, and ask God to make His truth known to us. God will make His truth known if we take the time to listen.

God Tells Us He is Self-Evident

If you allow God into your life, He will reveal His presence. There are times when God seems to be "more present." These are the times when we experience the presence of God in a more profound way. It is important to recognize these moments when His Spirit manifests in our daily lives.

The spiritual sense of experiencing God's present is something that calms your soul and at the same time, for a brief moment, lifts your spirit out of this mundane world. It is difficult to explain, but when it is experienced, it is not soon forgotten.

> Romans 1:19—They know the truth about God because he has made it obvious to them.

God's Invisible Attributes

We know there is one indivisible God. He is omniscient (all knowing), omnipresent (ever present), and omnipotent (all powerful). God is not just an invisible person or a spirit that embodies all things, but is the Father of all creation who lives in His spiritual kingdom which is within us and all around us. The embodiment of

His Spirit, the Holy Spirit, was given to us so that we can know Him and have a personal relationship with Him.

> Jeremiah 23:23–24—Am I a God who is only close at hand?" says the Lord. "No, I am far away at the same time. Can anyone hide from me in a secret place? Am I not everywhere in all the heavens and earth?" says the Lord.
>
> Matthew 18:20—For where two or three gather together as my followers, I am there among them."
>
> Deuteronomy 31:8—Do not be afraid or discouraged, for the Lord will personally go ahead of you. He will be with you; he will neither fail you nor abandon you.

God tells us that in His creation, His invisible attributes, can be clearly seen if our spiritual eyes are open. Sin is the greatest obstacle that blocks our spiritual sight.

> Isaiah 59:2—It's your sins that have cut you off from God. Because of your sins, he has turned away and will not listen anymore.
>
> Romans 3:23–24—For everyone has sinned; we all fall short of God's glorious standard. Yet God, in his grace, freely makes us right

in his sight. He did this through Christ Jesus when he freed us from the penalty for our sins.

Our Creator's invisible power and glory are so clearly seen in the things He has made that those of us who do not sense His presence are left without an excuse when it comes time for His righteous judgment.

> Romans 1:20—For ever since the world was created, people have seen the earth and sky. Through everything God made, they can clearly see his invisible qualities—his eternal power and divine nature. So they have no excuse for not knowing God.

> Psalms 139:8—If I go up to heaven, you are there; if I go down to the grave you are there.

- God is Omniscient—All Knowing.

> Psalms 147:4-5—He counts the stars and calls them all by name. How great is our Lord! His power is absolute! His understanding is beyond comprehension!

> Acts 15:18—He who made these things known so long ago.

> Psalms 33:13—The LORD looks down from heaven and sees the whole human race.

Isaiah 46:10—Only I (God) can tell you the future before it even happens. Everything I plan will come to pass, for I do whatever I wish.

Since God knows everything we do and our motives for doing them, we are to commit ourselves to do everything as if we were doing it for God. When I yield myself to Him daily, I find His will for my life and I become more of the person I know He wants me to be. It has been my experience that God is easy to love and easy to find as long as long as I include Him in my daily life.

- God is Omnipotent—All Powerful.

    Matthew 19:26—Jesus looked at them intently and said, "Humanly speaking, it is impossible. But with God everything is possible."

    John 1:3–5—God—created everything through him, and nothing was created except through him. The Word (Jesus) gave life to everything that was created, and his life brought light to everyone. The light shines in the darkness, and the darkness can never extinguish it.

    Luke 1:37—For the Word of God will never fail.

These scriptures tell us that if God says something will happen, He has the power to make it happen. Therefore, when He promises life in His eternal kingdom to those who believe in Him, He has the power to grant it. He cannot sin, but He has the power to forgive those who do.

Look for God's power in creation; majestic mountains, thunderstorms, gorgeous sunsets, beautiful flowers, rainbows and finally through the awesome knowledge of who you are. Scripture points out what many forget (but all know instinctively from birth), is that God is our heavenly Father.

- God is Omnipresent—Always Present.

    Proverbs 15:3—The Lord is watching everywhere, keeping his eye on both the evil and the good.

    Psalms 139:7–8—I can never escape from your Spirit! I can never get away from your presence! If I go up to heaven, you are there; if I go down to the grave (sheol), you are there.

    Job 34:21—"For God watches how people live; he sees everything they do.

To say God is omnipresent is to say that God is present everywhere at all times. Some religious systems teach that God is everywhere because He exists within His creation. This belief, called pantheism, says God is a part of the universe; trees, rocks, animals, stars, and people, are all part of God. The Bible teaches us that God exists outside of His creation. God is not in His Creation—His Creation is in Him.

One of the great mysteries of God is that He can be, in His entirety, there for each person at the same time. It is important to understand that God is totally present for each person. God does not give just a part of Himself to His children.

How God Communicates With Us

When the veil of this world is lifted, it is easy to see the different ways God reveals Himself to us. God communicates with everyone, not just Christians. When we wake our spiritual senses, the world where God lives comes alive in us. Below is a list of God's methods of communication. This list is not meant to be inclusive and will be discussed in more detail later.

- The Bible is God's Written Word.

    2 Timothy 3:16—All Scripture is inspired by God and is useful to teach us what is true and to make us realize what is wrong in our lives. It corrects us when we are wrong and teaches us to do what is right.

- The Quiet Inner Voice of the Holy Spirit.

    Psalms 40:10—I have not kept the good news of your justice hidden in my heart; I have talked about your faithfulness and saving power. I have told everyone in the great assembly of your unfailing love and faithfulness.

- The Advice and Counsel of Godly Men and Women.

    Proverbs 12:15—Fools think their own way is right, but the wise listen to others.

    Proverbs 19:2-21—Listen to advice and accept instruction, that you may gain wisdom in the future. Many are the plans in the mind of a man, but it is the purpose of the LORD that will stand.

- An Audible Voice.

    John 12:28—(Jesus prayed,) Father, bring glory to your name." Then a voice spoke from heaven, saying, "I have already brought glory to my name, and I will do so again."

A spiritual journey into the world where God lives

- In Dreams.

Genesis 31:11—Then in my dream, the angel of God said to me, 'Jacob!' And I replied, 'Yes, here I am.'

- In Visions.

Acts 9:10—Now there was a believer in Damascus named Ananias. The Lord spoke to him in a vision, calling, "Ananias!" "Yes, Lord!" he replied.

- By Angels.

Luke 1:26-33—In the sixth month of Elizabeth's pregnancy, God sent the angel Gabriel to Nazareth, a village in Galilee, to a virgin named Mary. She was engaged to be married to a man named Joseph, a descendant of King David. Gabriel appeared to her and said, "Greetings, favored woman! The Lord is with you!" Confused and disturbed, Mary tried to think what the angel could mean. "Don't be afraid, Mary," the angel told her, "for you have found favor with God! You will conceive and give birth to a son, and you will name him Jesus. He will be very great and will be called the Son of the Most High. The Lord God will give him the throne of his ancestor

David. And he will reign over Israel forever; his Kingdom will never end!"

- Through Life's Circumstances.

Jeremiah 29:11—For I know the plans I have for you," says the LORD. "They are plans for good and not for disaster, to give you a future and a hope.

Every person who now lives or has ever lived upon the face of the earth has heard from God. For many He is denied or just ignored.

How Do We Glorify God?

- We glorify Him in all we say, do, and think.
- We glorify Him by acknowledging Him to the world.
- We glorify Him by taking His love out into the world.
- We glorify Him by taking the message of His Son out into the world.
- We glorify Him with praise and worship.
- We glorify Him through our faith and trust.
- We glorify Him by following in the footsteps of His Son.
- We glorify Him by being obedient even unto death.
- We glorify Him by seeking His knowledge and wisdom.

- We glorify Him by aspiring to be like His Son.
- We glorify Him by being the person He wants us to be.
- We glorify Him by placing His desires and plans above our own.
- We glorify Him by taking the time to seek His presence.
- We glorify Him by caring for His creation.

2 Corinthians 3:18
So all of us who have had that veil removed can see and reflect the glory of the Lord. And the Lord—who is the Spirit—makes us more and more like him as we are changed into his glorious image.

Chapter Two

The Spirit of God

Psalm 139:7–10
I can never escape from your Spirit! I can never get away from your presence! If I go up to heaven, you are there; if I go down to the grave, you are there. If I ride the wings of the morning, if I dwell by the farthest oceans, even there your hand will guide me and your strength will support me.

God's Holy Spirit

The Bible does not give us a proper name for the Holy Spirit. The Scriptures tell us instead about His work, purpose and relationship with Man. The names used for the Holy Spirit are only a description of His power and purpose.

The following are some of the more common descriptive names of the Holy Spirit.

- The Spirit of God over the Earth.

    Genesis 1:2—The earth was formless and empty, and darkness covered the deep waters. And the Spirit of God was hovering over the surface of the waters.

- The Spirit of the Lord—Wisdom, Understanding, Counsel, Might, Knowledge.

    Isaiah 11:2—And the Spirit of the Lord will rest on him—the Spirit of wisdom and understanding, the Spirit of counsel and might, the Spirit of knowledge and the fear of the Lord.

- The Spirit of Good.

    Nehemiah 9:20—You sent your good Spirit to instruct them, and you did not stop giving them manna from heaven or water for their thirst.

- The Spirit of the Father.

    Matthew 10:20—For it is not you who will be speaking—it will be the Spirit of your Father speaking through you.

- The Spirit of Jesus Christ.

    Galatians 4:6—And because we are his children, God has sent the Spirit of his Son into our hearts, prompting us to call out, "Abba, Father."

    Philippians 1:19—For I know that as you pray for me and the Spirit of Jesus Christ helps me, this will lead to my deliverance.

- The Spirit of Truth.

    John 16:13—When the Spirit of truth comes, he will guide you into all truth. He will not speak on his own, but will tell you what he has heard. He will tell you about the future.

- The Spirit of Holiness.

    Romans 1:4—And he (Jesus) was shown to be (the Spirit of Holiness) the Son of God when he was raised from the dead by the power of the Holy Spirit. He is Jesus Christ our Lord.

- The Spirit of Life.

    Romans 8:2—And because you belong to him, the power of the life-giving Spirit has freed you from the power of sin that leads to death.

- The Spirit of Glory.

  1 Peter 4:14—If you are insulted because you bear the name of Christ, you will be blessed, for the glorious Spirit of God rests upon you.

- The Eternal Spirit.

  Hebrews 9:14—Just think how much more the blood of Christ will purify our consciences from sinful deeds so that we can worship the living God. For by the power of the eternal Spirit, Christ offered himself to God as a perfect sacrifice for our sins.

- The Spirit of Grace and Prayer.

  Zachariah 12:10—Then I will pour out a spirit of grace and prayer on the family of David and on the people of Jerusalem. They will look on me whom they have pierced, and mourn for him as for an only son. They will grieve bitterly for him as for a firstborn son who has died.

- The Spirit of Judgment.

    1 Corinthians 2:15—Those who are spiritual (have the Spirit of Judgement) can evaluate all things, but they themselves cannot be evaluated by others.

- The Spirit of Prophecy.

    Revelations 19:10—Then I fell down at his feet to worship him, but he said, "No, don't worship me. I am a servant of God, just like you and your brothers and sisters who testify about their faith in Jesus. Worship only God. For the essence (Spirit) of prophecy is to give a clear witness for Jesus."

- The Spirit of Wisdom and Insight.

    Ephesians 1:17—Asking God, the glorious Father of our Lord Jesus Christ, to give you spiritual wisdom and insight so that you might grow in your knowledge of God.

Indwelling of the Holy Spirit

Receiving the Holy Spirit is not only the greatest gift from God, but the presence of God indwelling makes available to all of us God's power, fullness and grace. For this reason, it is important we recognize and understand fully the Holy Spirit's true nature.

> 1 Corinthians 2:11–12—No one can know a person's thoughts except that person's own spirit, and no one can know God's thoughts except God's own Spirit. And we have received God's Spirit (not the world's spirit), so we can know the wonderful things God has freely given us.

The Holy Spirit came to lead us in the way of righteousness, make known the truth of God's Word, and guide us away from the errors of sin. He bestows upon believers a new nature—a spiritual nature. This new nature is able to transform the believer's heart, mind, and spirit. It is this new nature that opens us to the spiritual world.

> John 16:15—All that belongs to the Father is mine; this is why I said, 'The Spirit will tell you whatever he receives from me.'

> Romans 8:5—Those who are dominated by the sinful nature think about sinful things, but those who are controlled by the Holy Spirit think about things that please the Spirit.

The Spirit of God

Many believers after receiving the indwelling of the Holy Spirit just ignore His power, guidance, and teachings. They do not put into practice the power of the Spirit, the gifts of the Spirit, or the Fruit of the Spirit and then wonder why God does not seem to be there for them. It is not possible to be full of the Spirit and full of yourself at the same time. Believers are encouraged to accept the fullness of the Spirit and live under His power.

> Luke 11:11–13—"You fathers—if your children ask for a fish, do you give them a snake instead? Or if they ask for an egg, do you give them a scorpion? Of course not! So if you sinful people know how to give good gifts to your children, how much more will their heavenly Father give the Holy Spirit to those who ask him."

> Ephesians 5:15–21—So be careful how you live. Don't live like fools, but like those who are wise. Make the most of every opportunity in these evil days. Don't act thoughtlessly, but understand what the Lord wants you to do. Don't be drunk with wine, because that will ruin your life. Instead, be filled with the Holy Spirit, singing psalms and hymns and spiritual songs among yourselves, and making music to the Lord in your hearts. And give thanks for everything to God the

Father in the name of our Lord Jesus Christ. And further, submit to one another out of reverence for Christ.

Exodus 31:3—I have filled him (Moses) with the Spirit of God, giving him great wisdom, ability, and expertise in all kinds of crafts.

To be filled with the power of the Holy Spirit is to allow God to be a part of your choices, decisions, goals, desires, behavior, and in all other circumstances of your life. If you are growing as a believer, He will be there in all of your relationships: at work, home, church, or wherever you happen to be.

The Holy Spirit ~~Bares~~ Bears God's Truth

The Holy Spirit's main directive is to help us along our spiritual journey in a way we are not able to do on our own.

- The Holy Spirit encourages us to ~~bare~~ Bear Spiritual Fruit.

    Galatians 5:22-23—But the Holy Spirit produces this kind of fruit in our lives: love, joy, peace, patience, kindness, goodness, faithfulness, gentleness, and self-control. There is no law against these things!

- We are to be led by the Spirit.

    Galatians 5:25—Since we are living by the Spirit, let us follow the Spirit's leading (walk in the Spirit) in every part of our lives.

- We are to be filled with the Spirit.

    Ephesians 5:18—Don't be drunk with wine, because that will ruin your life. Instead, be filled with the Holy Spirit.

How the Holy Spirit Reveals Himself

The Holy Spirit also performs a function for unbelievers who want to know who God is. He convicts their hearts of God's truth concerning sin and the need for redemption. He shows them the truth of Jesus Christ—that He died on the cross in their place to release them from the bondage of Sin. He brings them to repentance and offers them a new life in Jesus Christ.

- From the first letter Paul sent to the Corinthians, we learn the Holy Spirit reveals to believers the things of God.

    1 Corinthians 2:10—But it was to us that God revealed these things by his Spirit. For his Spirit searches out everything and shows us God's deep secrets.

- From Psalm 33 we learn that the Lord spoke, and the heavens were created.

Psalms 33:6—The Lord merely spoke, and the heavens were created. He breathed the Word, and all the stars were born.

- From Paul's first letter to the Corinthians we learn that Man cannot understand the things of God without the guidance and direction of the Holy Spirit. If we use good judgment when discerning the voice of the Holy Spirit, His truth will be apparent.

1 Corinthians 2:14–16—But people who aren't spiritual can't receive these truths from God's Spirit. It all sounds foolish to them and they can't understand it, for only those who are spiritual can understand what the Spirit means. Those who are spiritual can evaluate all things, but they themselves cannot be evaluated by others. For, "Who can know the Lord's thoughts? Who knows enough to teach him?" But we understand these things, for we have the mind of Christ.

The Holy Spirit's Relationship Between God And Man

The Holy Spirit is co-equal with God the Father and God the Son. Without the Holy Spirit it is absolutely impossible to live a Christian life and to properly serve God. Yet few biblical doctrines about the power of the Holy Spirit have caused more confusion among Christians.

The Holy Spirit inspired men of God to write the biblical texts. As you read these texts, the Holy Spirit unfolds His truth and comes alive in you. You can read the same scripture over and over again and suddenly the next time you read it an unknown revelation reveals itself. Why does this happen? It is because God needs to make a particular truth known to you at a particular time. The Bible is the living Word of God and can only be known when God's Holy Spirit brings it alive in you. No person can properly interpret God's written Word without the Holy Spirit.

> 1 Corinthians 2:14—But people who aren't spiritual can't receive these truths from God's Spirit. It all sounds foolish to them and they can't understand it, for only those who are spiritual can understand what the Spirit means.

Satan does not want God's people to know and use the power of the Holy Spirit. He would like God's people to go through life struggling on their own and not recognizing the power available to them. I sometimes think Christians are afraid to call upon the Holy Spirit or they are saving His power for the difficult challenges of life. The Church to some degree has not emphasized or adequately explained the power and gifts available to its people through the Holy Spirit.

The Holy Spirit is the true power of the divine available to Man. The Holy Spirit:

- Anoints us for ministry.

    Luke 4:18—The Spirit of the Lord is upon me, for he has anointed me to bring Good News to the poor. He has sent me to proclaim that captives will be released, that the blind will see, that the oppressed will be set free.

- Testifies of our Lord and Savior Jesus Christ.

    John 15:26—But I will send you the Advocate—the Spirit of truth. He will come to you from the Father and will testify all about me.

    John 16:14-15—He will bring me glory by telling you whatever he receives from me. All that belongs to the Father is mine; this is why I (Jesus) said, 'The Spirit will tell you whatever He receives from me.'

- Guides us in all truth.

    John 16:13–16—When the Spirit of truth comes, he will guide you into all truth. He will not speak on his own, but will tell you what he has heard. He will tell you about the future. He will bring me glory by telling you whatever he receives from me. All that belongs to the Father is mine; this is why I said, 'The Spirit will tell you whatever he receives from me.' "In a little while you won't see me anymore. But a little while after that, you will see me again."

- Convicts us of Sin.

    John 16:8—And when he (Holy Spirit) comes, he will convict the world of its sin, and of God's righteousness, and of the coming judgment.

- Gives us gifts for ministry.

    1 Corinthians 12:11—It is the one and only Spirit who distributes all these gifts. He alone decides which gift each person should have.

    Hebrews 2:4—And God confirmed the message by giving signs and wonders and various

A spiritual journey into the world where God lives

miracles and gifts of the Holy Spirit whenever he chose.

- Gives us power to do the things Jesus commanded us to do.

Matthew 9:8—Fear swept through the crowd as they saw this happen. And they praised God for giving humans such authority.

- Teaches us what we should to say.

Luke 12:12—For the Holy Spirit will teach you at that time what needs to be said."

- Testifies to us the things of God.

Hebrews 10:15-16—And the Holy Spirit also testifies that this is so. For he says, "This is the new covenant I will make with my people on that day, says the Lord: I will put my laws in their hearts, and I will write them on their minds."

- Intercedes for us in prayer.

Romans 8:26-27—And the Holy Spirit helps us in our weakness. For example, we don't know what God wants us to pray for. But the Holy Spirit prays for us with groanings that cannot be expressed in words. And the Father who knows all hearts knows what the Spirit is saying, for the Spirit pleads for us believers in harmony with God's own will.

- Bear witness in us that we are His children.

    Romans 8:16—For his Spirit joins with our spirit to affirm that we are God's children.

- Reveals Himself to us.

    1 Corinthians 2:9–10—That is what the Scriptures mean when they say, "No eye has seen, no ear has heard, and no mind has imagined what God has prepared for those who love him." But it was to us that God revealed these things by his Spirit. For his Spirit searches out everything and shows us God's deep secrets.

- Speaks for us.

    1 Corinthians 2:13—When we tell you these things, we do not use words that come from human wisdom. Instead, we speak words given to us by the Spirit, using the Spirit's words to explain spiritual truths.

- Cleanses us from sin and renews our spirit.

> Titus 3:5—He (Jesus) saved us, not because of the righteous things we had done, but because of his mercy. He washed away our sins, giving us a new birth and new life through the Holy Spirit.

- Sanctifies us.

> 2 Thessalonians 2:13—As for us, we can't help but thank God for you, dear brothers and sisters loved by the Lord. We are always thankful that God chose you to be among the first to experience salvation—a salvation that came through the Spirit who makes you holy and through your belief in the truth.

- Gives us wisdom and knowledge.

> 1 Corinthians 12:8—To one person the Spirit gives the ability to give wise advice; to another the same Spirit gives a message of special knowledge.

Communicating with the Holy Spirit

The Holy Spirit is not something to be seen as just running in the background waiting to surface when you need Him. The Holy Spirit wants to be in the foreground communicating with you daily and to help in all aspects of your life. When you are not in constant contact with the Holy Spirit and seeking His advice, your flesh can easily override His voice. The Holy Spirit waits and wants to communicate with you.

To be able to see and hear what God reveals to us through His Holy Spirit, we need to go through a spiritual awakening process. As we open ourselves to the Holy Spirit, He comes alive in us, opening the spiritual world. When this happens our worldly ways begin to fade away and a new Spirit empowers us and the truth of the spiritual world becomes known.

With the awakening process, comes responsibility. You can tread along without embracing it or you can grasp its significance and recognize it as the most important step you have ever taken in your life. Only by embracing this emerging consciousness of God does He disclose Himself and become the driving force for spiritual growth.

The initiation of the awakening process is an act of God's grace through His Son Jesus Christ. This is why Jesus associated with all people, Jews and Gentiles, saints and sinners.

When the need for a power greater than our own is realized, God sees the desire of our heart and He draws us to Him. Once we begin to awaken to God's Spirit, we know it firsthand. It is no longer just a concept in our mind. Space for the spiritual has opened in our lives. People who have experienced this awakening process realize that what drives the natural world no longer drives them.

Awakening the Spirit in you is also a divine experience involving a realization or opening to a sacred dimension of reality, allowing the discernment of spiritual things. It offers a process of personal transformation that awakens and inspires us to recognize our true spiritual identity and our oneness with all life. The awakening process must be an individual quest or it has no meaning.

What Are You Feeding Your Spirit?

We feed our physical body three times a day and often with snacks in between. How often do we feed our spirit—our spiritual body? When we do not feed our spirit, our sinful nature may find its appetites more desirable. To go beyond our sinful nature we must seek out and make a part of our lives those things that feed our spiritual nature. When we nourish our spiritual self, we know there is something in us and out there that transcends the part of us that desires the things this world has to offer.

> Romans 7:18—And I (Paul) know that nothing good lives in me, that is, in my sinful nature. I want to do what is right, but I can't.

Have you ever thought about what you are feeding your spirit? Your spirit is fed by the things you dwell on in your mind. When love, praise, and thanksgiving dominate your thoughts, you can find joy even in the most difficult of circumstances. Yet when doubt, discouragement, depression or fear dominates your mind, your spirit can be dragged down to the point where you lose the capacity to make rational decisions. It is important to look at what path your thoughts travel. For your spirit to grow and blossom it must be fed spiritual food.

> John 6:63—The Spirit alone gives eternal life. Human effort accomplishes nothing. And the very words I (Jesus) have spoken to you are spirit and life.

- Feed your spirit each day with the divine nature of God in Creation.

> Romans 1:20—For ever since the world was created, people have seen the earth and sky. Through everything God made, they can clearly see his invisible qualities—his eternal power and divine nature. So they have no excuse for not knowing God.

- Feed your spirit each day with the living Word of God.

> John 6:50-51–Anyone who eats the bread from heaven, however, will never die. I am the living bread that came down from heaven. Anyone who eats this bread will live forever;

and this bread, which I will offer so the world may live, is my flesh."

1 Peter 2:1-3–So get rid of all evil behavior. Be done with all deceit, hypocrisy, jealousy, and all unkind speech. Like newborn babies, you must crave pure spiritual milk so that you will grow into a full experience of salvation. Cry out for this nourishment, now that you have had a taste of the Lord's kindness.

- Feed your spirit each day with the light of the Lord.

Ephesians 5:8–10—For once you were full of darkness, but now you have light from the Lord. So live as people of light! For this light within you produces only what is good and right and true. Carefully determine what pleases the Lord.

- Fill your spirit each day with living water.

John 4:10—Jesus replied, "If you only knew the gift God has for you and who you are speaking to, you would ask me, and I would give you living water."

- Feed your spirit each day with the bread of life.

    John 6:35—Jesus replied, "I am the bread of life. Whoever comes to me will never be hungry again. Whoever believes in me will never be thirsty.

- Feed your spirit each day with God's unfailing love.

    Psalms 48:9—O God, we meditate on your unfailing love as we worship in your Temple.

If you are insensitive to your spirit you will be unaware of the many awesome spiritual gifts available to you. Begin by paying close attention to your day-to-day life, recognizing the moments when you feel clear of mind and peacefully involved in what you are doing. Notice exactly what you are doing and focus on those activities that leave you with a sense of peace and self-satisfaction. Note what happens when you give God praise, help someone, smile, laugh, feel lighthearted, see something beautiful, or find yourself doing something that lifts your spirit beyond the ordinary. These are the daily moments when you are walking in the Spirit and your spirit is nurtured. These are the experiences that disconnect your mind from the natural world and connect you to the spiritual world. Be very aware of how you feel in these moments when your spirit is being nurtured.

If you do not know where to begin, do not worry. If you genuinely want to awaken your spirit, all it requires is listening to, and spending quality time with God. You will know you are in the presence of God when you are aware of that quietness inside of you and when you feel at peace, loved, contented, compassionate and lighthearted.

One great way to nurture your spirit is to leave a free period of time each day when you can be alone with God and answer to no one but yourself. Pursue one of your passions such as spending time in the garden, reading a good book or simply relaxing over a cup of tea or coffee. Some of the ways to nurture your spirit are:

- Spending quality time with loved ones.
- Spending quality time with God.
- Planting and caring for a garden.
- Listening to music that stirs your soul.
- Learning new things about God.
- Breathing in fresh air.
- Being creative.
- Singing gospel hymns.
- Taking a leisurely walk in the woods.
- Spending time by the ocean or a river.
- Watching children or animals play.
- Receiving a hug.
- Watching a sunset or a sunrise.
- Helping someone.
- Having a really enjoyable meal.
- Caring for a beloved pet.
- Listening to the rain.
- Meditating on God's Word.

- Quietly observing nature.
- Sitting by a waterfall.
- Being on the receiving end of a smile.
- Buying something you like, not something you need.
- Having a quiet time.
- Smelling the fragrance of a flower.
- Sensing the beauty in the things around you.
- Spending quality time with a child.

God is Always There For You

One of the mysteries of God is that He is an infinite Spirit and is everywhere in each moment of time. He will come to live in you if you lay your sins at the foot of the cross.

The universe is filled with His glory and all of His divine personal attributes: love, joy, peace, kindness, gentleness, goodness, faithfulness, and forbearance. These attributes are there for you and me, all we have to do is make them a part of our life.

- We live in God when we walk in His Spirit.

    Acts 17:28—For in him we live and move and exist. As some of your own poets have said, 'We are his offspring.'

    John 15:4-5–Remain in me, and I will remain in you. For a branch cannot produce fruit if it is severed from the vine, and you cannot be fruitful unless you remain in me. "Yes, I am the vine; you are the branches. Those who remain in me, and I in them, will produce much fruit. For apart from me you can do nothing.

- We are to live as Jesus did.

1 John 2:6—Those who say they live in God should live their lives as Jesus did.

- As children of God we walk in His light.

Ephesians 5:8—For once you were full of darkness, but now you have light from the Lord. So live as people of light!

- As children of God, we are to walk in His love.

Ephesians 5:2—Live a life filled with love, following the example of Christ. He loved us and offered himself as a sacrifice for us, a pleasing aroma to God.

- We are to bare witness to the truth of Jesus.

John 18:37—Pilate said, "So you are a king?" Jesus responded, "You say I am a king. Actually, I was born and came into the world to testify to the truth. All who love the truth recognize that what I say is true."

- We are to worship God in spirit and truth.

    John 4:24—For God is Spirit, so those who worship him must worship in spirit and in truth."

We live within His grace and divine presence every moment of every day. God knows everything we say and do. When we do something good God sees it, when we do something bad God sees it.

The Apostle Paul tells us:

> Hebrews 4:13—Nothing in all creation is hidden from God. Everything is naked and exposed before his eyes, and he is the one to whom we are accountable.

> 1 Corinthians 3:16—Don't you realize that all of you together are the Temple of God and that the Spirit of God lives in you?

It is important to understand that our spiritual nature seeks truth, and our sinful nature is abusive and destructive. Our spiritual nature has within it the Fruit of the Spirit, including empowerment, empathy, unity, and creativity among many other positive virtues. This is the nature that works for the good in us and inclines us to see the good in others and in the world around us. Our sinful nature inclines us towards wrong desires and draws us towards the wickedness of a fallen world. The one we feed becomes dominant in our life.

God wants us to "consciously" live in His presence each day. His ever-presence makes it possible for us to be in constant communication with Him and to know His will in every situation. But too often we ignore His presence because we are so preoccupied with our self-centered lives, we just forget He is there.

Yet, God's divine presence is all we need for any challenge that may come our way. He is always there, hearing our prayers, protecting us and watching over us. God is our ever-present Savior and Lord.

> Matthew 28:20—Teach these new disciples to obey all the commands I (Jesus) have given you. And be sure of this: I am with you always, even to the end of the age."

Two Wolves—A Cherokee Legend

One evening an old Cherokee told his grandson about a battle that goes on inside people. He said, "My son, the battle is between two 'wolves' inside us all. One is Evil. It is anger, envy, jealousy, sorrow, regret, greed, arrogance, self-pity, guilt, worry, resentment, inferiority, lies, false pride, superiority, and ego. The other is good. It is joy, peace, love, hope, serenity, humility, kindness, benevolence, empathy, humor, generosity, truth, compassion and faith." The grandson thought for a minute and then asked his grandfather, "Which wolf wins?" The old Cherokee simply replied, "The one you feed."

Reprinted and used by permission- lifeway.com

Romans 8:9–10
But you are not controlled by your sinful nature. You are controlled by the Spirit if you have the Spirit of God living in you. (And remember that those who do not have the Spirit of Christ living in them do not belong to him). And Christ lives within you, so even though your body will die because of sin, the Spirit gives you life because you have been made right with God.

Chapter Three

Are You Listening?

Proverbs 2:1–5

My child, listen to what I say, and treasure my commands. Tune your ears to wisdom, and concentrate on understanding. Cry out for insight, and ask for understanding. Search for them as you would for silver; seek them like hidden treasures. Then you will understand what it means to fear the Lord, and you will gain knowledge of God.

Are You Ready to Listen?

We must always be conscious of God in our daily lives and listen to His voice so that our spiritual awareness never fades, and our spiritual hearing never becomes dull. It is a law of life that we only see what we focus on and hear what we have been trained to hear. Only the person who has developed the ability to see and hear in the spiritual world will be knowingly aware of God's presence.

Seeing and hearing God is something we should all long for. It is not hard to do; in fact, God wants us to see and hear Him. Seeing and hearing God can become as natural as seeing and hearing our best friends.

Seeing Into and Hearing From the Spiritual World

Every Christian is gifted to discern the presence of God, hear His voice and follow His guidance. As sons and daughters of God's Kingdom, we have been given the spiritual sight to see and the spiritual ears to hear the things of God.

> 2 Corinthians 4:3-4—If the Good News we preach is hidden behind a veil, it is hidden only from people who are perishing. Satan, who is the god of this world, has blinded the minds of those who don't believe. They are unable to see the glorious light of the Good News. They don't understand this message about the glory of Christ, who is the exact likeness of God.

> Proverbs 20:12—Ears to hear and eyes to see—both are gifts from the LORD.

> Acts 26:17-18—And I (Jesus) will rescue you from both your own people and the Gentiles. Yes, I am sending you to the Gentiles to open their eyes, so they may turn from darkness to light and from the power of Satan to God. Then they will receive forgiveness for their sins and be given a place among God's people, who are set apart by faith in me.'

Jesus declared that all His sheep hear His voice, not just a chosen few. God created you to experience His love and to know His voice.

> John 10:27—My sheep listen to my voice; I know them, and they follow me.

> Ephesians 1:13–14—And now you Gentiles have also heard the truth, the Good News that God saves you. And when you believed in Christ, he identified you as his own by giving you the Holy Spirit, whom he promised long ago. The Spirit is God's guarantee that he will give us the inheritance he promised and that he has purchased us to be his own people. He did this so we would praise and glorify him.

When Scripture is interpreted through the Spirit of Jesus Christ, it leads us into a living relationship with the

Father. When we hear the voice of the Living Word, we receive spiritual knowledge.

> Hebrews 11:3—By faith we understand that the entire universe was formed at God's command, that what we now see did not come from anything that can be seen.
>
> John 16:13–15—When the Spirit of truth comes, he will guide you into all truth. He will not speak on his own, but will tell you what he has heard. He will tell you about the future. He will bring me glory by telling you whatever he receives from me. All that belongs to the Father is mine; this is why I said, 'The Spirit will tell you whatever he receives from me.'
>
> 2 Corinthians 4:6—For God, who said, "Let there be light in the darkness," has made this light shine in our hearts so we could know the glory of God that is seen in the face of Jesus Christ.

The Things of God Are Spiritually Discerned

Along our life's journey, there are many potential pitfalls and sidetracks. Without God's guidance, there are many ways to misinterpret what we are experiencing, to get stuck at some point and to cease growing spiritually.

Or worse yet, we might follow the ways of the natural world and destroy any chance we have of receiving the awesome things God has for us to see and hear.

> 1 Corinthians 2:11–14—No one can know a person's thoughts except that person's own spirit, and no one can know God's thoughts except God's own Spirit. And we have received God's Spirit (not the world's spirit), so we can know the wonderful things God has freely given us. When we tell you these things, we do not use words that come from human wisdom. Instead, we speak words given to us by the Spirit, using the Spirit's words to explain spiritual truths. But people who aren't spiritual can't receive these truths from God's Spirit. It all sounds foolish to them and they can't understand it, for only those who are spiritual can understand what the Spirit means.

> Ephesians 1:17—Asking God, the glorious Father of our Lord Jesus Christ, to give you spiritual wisdom and insight so that you might grow in your knowledge of God.

It is important to understand that it is possible to harden your heart to a point where God lets you go your own way and leaves you to live without Him.

> Ephesians 4:18—Their minds are full of darkness; they wander far from the life God gives because they have closed their minds and hardened their hearts against him.

> Matthew 13:14–15—This fulfills the prophecy of Isaiah that says, When you hear what I say, you will not understand. When you see what I do, you will not comprehend. For the hearts of these people are hardened, and their ears cannot hear and they have closed their eyes—so their eyes cannot see, and their ears cannot hear, and their hearts cannot understand, and they cannot turn to me and let me heal them.

Who Am I Listening To?

"Who am I listening to" is an important question. Peter's great confession that Jesus was the Son of God, came to him through the Holy Spirit.

> Matthew 16:17—Jesus replied, "You are blessed, Simon son of John, because my Father in heaven has revealed this to you. You did not learn this from any human being.

We are instructed to test the spirits to see whether they are from God, or not. This also applies to the voices we hear telling us what choices to make. We should test these voices to know their origin. Knowing the origin of each of the different voices we hear allows us to discern the speaker.

> John 10:27—My sheep listen to my voice; I know them, and they follow me. I give them eternal life, and they will never perish. No one can snatch them away from me.

The above scripture tells us we can know God's voice from others. Those who belong to God's family can learn to recognize the voice of God because God is their heavenly Father. To know implies an intimate family relationship with and not just an intellectual knowledge of. This is the same phenomenon that occurs when a child knows the voice of his parents. There is an intimate relationship that develops. The child knows its parent's voice even if the parent cannot be seen.

Why would we want to hear God's voice? This may sound like a silly question, but motivation (desire and intent) is important in anything we do.

> Hebrews 4:12—For the Word of God is alive and powerful. It is sharper than the sharpest two-edged sword, cutting between soul and spirit, between joint and marrow. It exposes our innermost thoughts and desires.

A radio can tune in and make unheard signals audible. When we hear the sounds coming from a radio they become real to us, but the sounds were already there before we tuned in. A radio does not generate sounds—it just receives signals and converts them into sounds we can hear.

The greatest challenge we face when we want to hear God's voice is tuning out all the other voices we hear during the day. Not being able to discern God's voice and then listening to the wrong voice can have dire consequences. All you have to do is look at all the false prophets that have not only destroyed their lives, but also the lives of those who have believed and acted on their teaching.

Think about all the people who are so hungry for God's Word that they blindly follow a false prophet. Those who do not spend time in the Bible to know God's Word are easily led astray. They follow a false teaching instead of God's voice. You need to get in the Word of God and stay there.

> 2 Peter 2:1—But there were also false prophets in Israel, just as there will be false teachers among you. They will cleverly teach destructive heresies and even deny the Master who bought them. In this way, they will bring sudden destruction on themselves.

> John 8:31–32—Jesus said to the people who believed in him, "You are truly my disciples if you remain faithful to my teachings. And

> you will know the truth, and the truth will set you free."

As an example of false prophets, look at all the ministers of God who prophesied the date for the coming of the end of the world. I believe they honestly thought it was a word of knowledge from God. Not only was their ministry discredited or destroyed, but what about the lives of those who worked for the ministry or the lives of those who gave up everything to follow them. What about the unbelievers who saw them make fools out of themselves? Do they not know that God's Word speaks loud and clear?

> Matthew 24:36—"However, no one knows the day or the hour when these things will happen, not even the angels in heaven or the Son himself. Only the Father knows.

Never (never, never, never) accept a word of knowledge from the voices you hear or from someone who has prophesied in God's name unless you have confirmed it in the Word of God. Make sure there is no doubt as to its authenticity. An incorrect word of knowledge or prophecy can have far-reaching implications.

> Acts 17:11—And the people of Berea were more open-minded than those in Thessalonica, and they listened eagerly to Paul's message.

> They searched the Scriptures day after day to
> see if Paul and Silas were teaching the truth.

We must pray daily for God to ingrain His Word of truth in us. We must seek after the filling of His Spirit to enlighten our hearts and to guide us in all truth. It is not enough to rely on theological dogma because its teaching is only valid if it is taught in the truth of God's Word. We must go to the Bible ourselves, read it, study it, and ask God to make His voice known to us. God will make His voice known if we take the time to listen.

Discerning the Difference between the Voices We Hear

Hundreds of thoughts enter in and out of your mind every day, some consciously and some subconsciously. Knowing the source of the voices you hear is challenging, but also crucial to not be trapped in a life where you are not in control of your own destiny. Every choice you make is according to the voice you listen to.

> Isaiah 30:18, 21—So the LORD must wait for you to come to him so he can show you his love and compassion. For the LORD is a faithful God. Blessed are those who wait for his help . . . Your own ears will hear him. Right behind you a voice will say. "This is the way you should go," whether to the right or to the left.

God's voice always speaks of love, even in times of adversity His love is there. Have you heard people say, "The Lord told me this or the Lord told me that?" How did they know it was God speaking to them, or was it God?

First, you have to know God's voice. You have to be able to recognize God's voice from among others. Consider the following scripture:

> Isaiah 55:11—It is the same with my Word. I send it out, and it always produces fruit. It will accomplish all I want it to, and it will prosper everywhere I send it.

> Romans 12:2—Don't copy the behavior and customs of this world, but let God transform you into a new person by changing the way you think. Then you will learn to know God's will for you, which is good and pleasing and perfect.

Ideally, all the voices you hear would be prefaced with, "This message is from God," "You are about to hear from Satan," or "This is yourself speaking." Unfortunately, it does not work that way. Identifying the source of a voice can be learned and is necessary for living a Christian life.

God will never lead you down the wrong path. If you find yourself on the wrong path, know that the voice of God did not lead you there. Begin by always basing the voice you hear on the following questions:

- Does it feel kind and loving?
- Does it consider the feelings of everyone involved?
- Is the guidance trustworthy and non-threatening?
- Does it help me without the possibility of hurting anyone else?
- Is it in accordance with God's Word?

If you can answer "Yes" to all of these questions, then the voice you are hearing is worth considering. It is also important to recognize the difference between true guidance and wishful thinking. True guidance (God's quiet voice) is subtle and considers everyone who may be involved and will always lead you along the high road of personal responsibility, spiritual growth, and integrity. True guidance will not leave you with second thoughts, such as buying something you cannot afford and later regretting it.

The three most important voices you need to recognize are the voice of God, the voice of your flesh and the voice of Satan. The voice of your flesh (sin in your body) and the voice of Satan are difficult to separate, so I am going to treat them as the same voice.

How God Speaks to Us Today

Consider that every choice we make in life is based on the voice we listen to. How do we discern the correct voice for making the right choice? This is where we need to see the importance of God's guiding voice in our lives. God helps us by talking to us in ways we can understand.

First, we are going to focus on the different ways God speaks to us. Later, we will discuss how to distinguish God's voice from others.

> Job 33:14—For God speaks again and again, though people do not recognize it.

God is not limited in any way. He is not restricted to certain methods of communication. Just as God communicated with a donkey, He can just as dramatically communicate His message to you.

> Numbers 22:28—Then the LORD gave the donkey the ability to speak. "What have I done to you that deserves your beating me three times?" it asked Balaam.

-God Speaks to Us Through His Word-

God's Word sometimes gives us a warning, a word of encouragement, or a lesson for life. This means He is sometimes whispering, and sometimes shouting as He gives us instructions and principles for living Spirit-filled lives. As we interpret scripture within its context and by other relevant scripture, we avoid the false logic and misinterpretations that can creep into our lives. If someone claims, "God told me to lie about my neighbor. Would you believe him? Of course not! God never violates His own Word. That "voice" did not come from God.

Are You Listening?

If you believe it is God speaking to you, know that God will tell you the same thing many times in different ways, and it will never contradict His written Word. Not only are we to have a growing relationship with God through His Word, but we also should be ready to give voice to His Word when necessary.

> 2 Timothy 3:16—All Scripture is inspired by God and is useful to teach us what is true and to make us realize what is wrong in our lives. It corrects us when we are wrong and teaches us to do what is right.

> 1 Peter 3:15—Instead, you must worship Christ as Lord of your life. And if someone asks about your hope as a believer, always be ready to explain it.

We must know God's expectations, and put into practice the truth of His Word. Knowing, honoring, and obeying God's commandments, is the key to hearing His voice.

> John 14:21, 23-24—Those who accept my commandments and obey them are the ones who love me. And because they love me, my Father will love them. And I will love them and reveal myself to each of them." . . . Jesus replied, "All who love me will do what I say. My Father will love them, and we will come and

make our home with each of them. Anyone who doesn't love me will not obey me. And remember, my words are not my own. What I am telling you is from the Father who sent me."

-God Speaks to Us Through Spiritual Encounters-

A spiritual event is one that invokes the extraordinary: a beautiful encounter, a breathtaking experience, a meaningful smile, a peace beyond measure, a quietness that calms your soul, or any circumstance that lifts your spirit beyond the ordinary.

One common thing we see in the examples of those who have had encounters with God is that these spiritual events were intensely real and significant to them.

An example is Paul's divine encounter on the road to Damascus. His encounter with Jesus was so intense that Paul's acceptance of Him was immediate. This profound event was critical in establishing the foundational tenets of Christianity. Of the twenty-seven books of the New Testament thirteen are ascribed to the Apostle Paul.

-God Speaks to Us Through Our Feelings-

Feelings are the subtlest form of communication we share with one another. They are much more discreet than words. They bypass our mind and connect with our innermost being. Growing up, many of us were taught that feelings are not very important, that true insight arrives through reason and intellect.

Although this is partly true, I have learned that feelings are as important, and sometimes more important than reason or knowledge, especially during times of discernment.

Christians often mistakenly assume that when they feel uplifted during a divine event that the feeling comes from the event itself. They will say something like, "The service was so inspiring" or "I loved the way the Pastor presented the life of Isaiah." We might say "I enjoyed the meal we had last night," or "the view of the sunset was so intensely beautiful."

That is, we either ascribe a good feeling to an external event, someone else, or something we do. We are affected by our outside environment, but feelings come from the inside. Events only trigger our emotions. It is our perception of an event that determines what we feel at any given moment. Our perception of an event can invoke the music of the soul or the torment of hell. Of all the paths, we travel in our lifetime feelings cause the most wonderful or terrifying experiences. Feelings have no boundaries, the depths can destroy us and the heights can bring us joy that transcends the world we live in.

There are feelings we experience that seem to have no apparent cause. It is these feelings we need to pay special attention to. It may be a sense of dread that is telling us to change our direction or a peaceful feeling of love when an angel is nearby. Learn to give these feelings special conscious recognition.

-God Speaks to Us Through Our Moral Compass-

The knowledge of right and wrong that God ingrained in us is monitored by our conscience. Our moral compass leads us to godly awareness and discernment.

Jeremiah 31:33—But this is the new covenant I will make with the people of Israel on that day," says the LORD. "I will put my instructions deep within them, and I will write them on their hearts. I will be their God, and they will be my people.

Ezekiel 36:26–27—Then I will sprinkle clean water on you, and you will be clean. Your filth will be washed away, and you will no longer worship idols. And I will give you a new heart, and I will put a new spirit in you. I will take out your stony, stubborn heart and give you a tender, responsive heart. And I will put my Spirit in you so that you will follow my decrees and be careful to obey my regulations.

1 Timothy 1:5—The purpose of my instruction is that all believers would be filled with love that comes from a pure heart, a clear conscience, and genuine faith.

-God Speaks to Us Through His Holy Spirit-

Why do you suppose a congregation can hear a sermon, but some people will walk away with a different truth that applies to them? In some cases, the preacher never spoke a word of what the people say they heard. Many times, it is the result of God's Spirit speaking a personal Word of truth to their spirits. It is when Scripture comes alive in us because it is "God-breathed."

> Revelation 3:20—Look! I stand at the door and knock. If you hear my voice and open the door, I will come in, and we will share a meal together as friends.

-God Speaks to Us Through His Creation-

God tells us He is evident in His creation and that if we open our spiritual eyes and ears to see and hear the things He has created, He becomes self-evident. God will never force us to listen to Him, but waits for our willing response to His call.

Have you ever felt indescribable joy, peace, or calmness of spirit while observing the awesome wonders of creation? Most of us have experienced this remarkable sense of God's presence in His creation at one time or another. It may have happened while lying on a beach and feeling the breeze of warm salt air, feeling the breathtaking sights while hiking in the mountains, sensing the fragrance of a flower, observing nature while walking through the woods, or while catching a glimpse of a beautiful sunset.

If everyone who has had these revelations were to look at these personal experiences as a disclosure of their Creator, they would begin to see a God who is loving, and powerful enough to bring to us such inspiring, dynamic, and beautiful encounters.

> Romans 1:20—For ever since the world was created, people have seen the earth and sky. Through everything God made, they can clearly see his invisible qualities—his eternal power and divine nature. So they have no excuse for not knowing God.

-God Speaks to Us Through Other People-

God may use a preacher, a friend, a teacher, a parent, or even an ungodly person to speak His message to us. These words may come as a warning, a blessing, or as a prophetic truth. One of the best places to find someone who can give you godly counsel is your local church. God will often direct you personally through the input of others who are regularly in Christian fellowship with you.

> James 3:17—But the wisdom from above is first of all pure. It is also peace loving, gentle at all times, and willing to yield to others. It is full of mercy and the fruit of good deeds. It shows no favoritism and is always sincere.

The Bible records many instances where God used one individual to deliver His message to another.

> 1 Samuel 13:13—"How foolish!" Samuel exclaimed. "You have not kept the command the LORD your God gave you. Had you kept it, the LORD would have established your kingdom over Israel forever.

> Acts 9:17—So Ananias went and found Saul. He laid his hands on him and said, "Brother Saul, the Lord Jesus, who appeared to you on the road, has sent me so that you might regain your sight and be filled with the Holy Spirit."

-God Speaks to Us Through Music-

One of the greatest ways to sense God's presence and hear His voice is when we praise Him with music. Praise brings an instant connection to the Holy Spirit. The power of the words and musical notes opens our heart and can lift our spirits to a divine level. King Jehoshaphat was facing a mighty army that could have destroyed His kingdom. But for some reason he decided to send out a choir of singers praising God with song.

> 2 Chronicles 20:21—After consulting the people, the king appointed singers to walk ahead of the army, singing to the Lord and praising him for his holy splendor. This is

what they sang: "Give thanks to the Lord; his faithful love endures forever!"

Ephesians 5:18-19—Don't be drunk with wine, because that will ruin your life. Instead, be filled with the Holy Spirit, singing psalms and hymns and spiritual songs among yourselves, and making music to the Lord in your hearts.

-God Speaks to Us Through Life's Circumstances-

People can hear God through their daily circumstances. God often uses events, good or bad to get our attention. When we learn to see God in the circumstances of life (good or bad), we need to give Him praise.

1 Thessalonians 5:18—Be thankful in all circumstances, for this is God's will for you who belong to Christ Jesus.

Romans 8:28—And we know that God causes everything to work together for the good of those who love God and are called according to his purpose for them.

-God Speaks to Us Through Prayer-

Unfortunately, many of us have the mistaken idea that the purpose of prayer is just to talk with God or petition Him with our wish list. Prayer is meant to bind our relationship with God and to know His will. At times, while we pray, God's Spirit will remind us of a scripture or a truth of His Word we can directly apply to the situation. Listen for God's quiet voice.

God always answers our prayer petitions, but unfortunately it is not always the answer we want or we may not even recognize the answer when it comes. Answer to prayer will come in God's time, not ours. Look for answers, prayer is a two-way street.

> Philippians 4:6—Don't worry about anything; instead, pray about everything. Tell God what you need, and thank him for all he has done.

When we do not know how to put our true feelings into words the Holy Spirit helps us in our weakness. The Holy Spirit intercedes for us through wordless groans that God understands.

> Romans 8:26–27—And the Holy Spirit helps us in our weakness. For example, we don't know what God wants us to pray for. But the Holy Spirit prays for us with groanings that cannot be expressed in words. And

the Father who knows all hearts knows what the Spirit is saying, for the Spirit pleads for us believers in harmony with God's own will.

-God Speaks to Us Through the Life of His Son-

The New Testament was the fulfillment of God's special plan for the redemption of Man. It's the gospel (the good news) of Jesus Christ.

> Hebrews 1:1-2—Long ago God spoke many times and in many ways to our ancestors through the prophets. And now in these final days, he has spoken to us through his Son. God promised everything to the Son as an inheritance, and through the Son he created the universe.

Through the words of Jesus in Scripture, we can "hear" the heart of God. These words were not written for a few select individuals, but were written for everyone for all time. We, as believers are to live out the life of Jesus.

-God Speaks to Us Through Dreams and Visions-

From Genesis to Revelation, God has spoken to people through dreams and visions. We can choose to invite God's Holy Spirit to open our eyes to the spiritual world through dreams and visions or we can just ignore it. Just as the prophets and visionaries of old, we as believers are today able to have spiritual dreams and visions.

God has not limited us to know Him only by His Word or by our intellect. We can see His work in the world around us and we can see in His world through dreams and visions. We can see God in everything that is real. When we put our spiritual lenses on there is no place where we will not see God.

The bottom line is that God loves us unconditionally and will spare no expense to get through to us.

James Dillet Freeman (1912–2003) was an internationally acclaimed poet, author, and lecturer. In 1971, a microfilm copy of Freeman's poem, "I Am There" was left on the moon by Apollo XV Astronaut James B. Irwin.

I Am There

You cannot see Me, yet I am the light you see by.
You cannot hear Me, yet I speak through your voice.
You cannot feel Me, yet I am the power at work in
your hands.
I am at work, though you do not understand My ways.
I am at work, though you do not understand
My works.
I am not strange visions. I am not mysteries.
Only in absolute stillness, beyond self, can
you know Me
as I AM, and then but as a feeling and a faith.

Yet I am here. Yet I hear. Yet I answer.
When you need ME, I am there.
Even if you deny Me, I am there.
Even when you feel most alone, I am there.
Even in your fears, I am there.
Even in your pain, I am there.
I am there when you pray and when you do not pray.
I am in you, and you are in Me.
Only in your mind can you feel separate from Me, for only in your mind are the mists of "yours" and "mine."
Yet only with your mind can you know Me and experience Me.
Empty your heart of empty fears.
When you get yourself out of the way, I am there.
You can of yourself do nothing, but I can do all.
And I AM in all.
Though you may not see the good, good is there, for I am there. I am there because I have to be, because I AM.
Only in Me does the world have meaning; only out of Me does the world take form; only because of ME does the world go forward.
I am the law on which the movement of the stars and the growth of living cells are founded.
I am the love that is the law's fulfilling. I am assurance.
I am peace. I am oneness. I am the law that you can live by.
I am the love that you can cling to. I am your assurance.
I am your peace. I am ONE with you. I am.
Though you fail to find ME, I do not fail you.

Though your faith in Me is unsure, My faith in you never
wavers, because I know you, because I love you.
Beloved, I AM there.

Used with permission of Unity (www.unity.org)

Ecclesiastes 3:1-8

For everything there is a season, a time for every activity under heaven. A time to be born and a time to die. A time to plant and a time to harvest. A time to kill and a time to heal. A time to tear down and a time to build up. A time to cry and a time to laugh. A time to grieve and a time to dance. A time to scatter stones and a time to gather stones. A time to embrace and a time to turn away. A time to search and a time to quit searching. A time to keep and a time to throw away. A time to tear and a time to mend. A time to be quiet and a time to speak. A time to love and a time to hate. A time for war and a time for peace.

Chapter Four

Our Spiritual Senses

1 Corinthians 2:14
But people who aren't spiritual can't receive these truths from God's Spirit. It all sounds foolish to them and they can't understand it, for only those who are spiritual can understand what the Spirit means.

Setting Your Sights on Heaven

Scripture makes it clear that we are to set our sights on heaven by surrendering our lives over to God. We are to concentrate on spiritual things that really matter, not on things of this world that have no real value.

> Colossians 3:1–2—Since you have been raised to new life with Christ, set your sights on the realities of heaven, where Christ sits in the place of honor at God's right hand. Think

about the things of heaven, not the things of earth.

Is it possible to live in both the spirit and the flesh at the same time? Scripture says yes. As long as we live in our physical body there will be times of despair and doubt, but we will not be controlled or consumed by it as long as we follow in the footsteps of our Lord and Savior Jesus Christ. The temptation to sin is usually presented through one or more of our five physical senses; therefore, it's important for us to recognize how this can happen. The Apostle Paul's ambition was to always do what was righteous and good, but because of the sin born in him he knew there would be times when he would fall short.

> Romans 7:18—And I know that nothing good lives in me, that is, in my sinful nature. I want to do what is right, but I can't.

C.S. Lewis "Mere Christianity" (p. 143)

> "A silly idea is current that good people do not know what temptation means. This is an obvious lie. Only those who try to resist temptation know how strong it is . . . A man who gives in to temptation after five minutes simply does not know what it would have been like an hour later. That is why bad people, in one sense, know very little about

badness. They have lived a sheltered life by always giving in."

Our Spiritual Senses

Most of us go through everyday life without giving much thought to our physical senses as we are so used to using them. As Christians, we need to raise the bar on our sensory awareness and allow both our physical and spiritual senses to guide and direct our path.

The same basic definition of physical senses can be applied to spiritual senses: sight, sound, smell, taste, touch. Our five physical senses are our means of navigating a material world. It is the same with our five spiritual senses, without them we would not be able to navigate a spiritual world.

What all this means is that we have in our spirit the five senses by which we can know the spiritual world as certainly as we know the physical world. Our spiritual senses are the faculties through which God interacts with us. If one or two of our physical senses are missing, then our experience of everyday life would be limited. It is the same with our spiritual senses; if one or two are missing our experience in our spiritual life would also be limited. Therefore, we have the responsibility to maintain our spiritual senses in good working order so we receive clear godly information.

-The Spiritual Sense of Sight-

From Genesis to Revelations, God has spoken to His people through dreams and visions. Seeing the spiritual world is a biblical concept that has continued throughout Church history and is prevalent in many churches today.

> Matthew 6:22—(Jesus said) "Your eye is like a lamp that provides light for your body. When your eye is healthy, your whole body is filled with light.

Just as blindness and deafness are serious handicaps in this world, so are spiritual blindness and deafness in the spiritual world. The spiritual world is all around us and is in many ways more real than the physical world. Many Christians do not know that by opening their spiritual eyes, they can see and interact with a spiritual world. Once your eyes are open, you will receive revelations you never dreamed possible.

Most Christians are spiritually blind when they begin their journey. They do not understand that the divine anointing of spiritual sight is available to all who seek it.

> Numbers 24:4—The message of one who hears the words of God, who sees a vision from the Almighty, who bows down with eyes wide open:

> 2 Kings 6:17—Then Elisha prayed, "O Lord, open his eyes and let him see!" The Lord opened the young man's eyes, and when he looked up, he saw that the hillside around Elisha was filled with horses and chariots of fire.

Roughly one-third of the human brain is devoted to visual processing. Our eyes have more sense receptors than the other four senses combined. This helps to explain the importance of seeing in our assessment and comprehension of the natural world. It is the same for the spiritual world. Spiritual sight allows us to assess and comprehend the spiritual world.

Throughout the world, many of God's people have spiritual dreams and visions that give them insight into the will of God. The following are just a few examples of the many biblical scriptures that show how God has in the past communicated with His people through dreams and visions.

> Ezekiel 1:1—On July 31 of my thirtieth year, while I was with the Judean exiles beside the Kebar River in Babylon, the heavens were opened and I saw visions of God.

> Genesis 28:12—As he slept, he dreamed of a stairway that reached from the earth up to heaven. And he saw the angels of God going up and down the stairway.

> Numbers 12:6—And the Lord said to them, "Now listen to what I say: "If there were prophets among you, I, the Lord, would reveal myself in visions. I would speak to them in dreams.

> Daniel 2:19—That night the secret was revealed to Daniel in a vision. Then Daniel praised the God of heaven.

-The Spiritual Sense of Hearing-

Throughout the Bible, we see time and time again where Jesus is speaking, and the Church does not have ears to hear. The Church is those of us who are supposed to walk with Jesus and know His voice.

God is always speaking to us, but most of the time we are not listening. One way to hear God's voice is learning to silence the noises that clutter our mind. During meditation or prayer try to keep random thoughts to a minimum and let the light of God's peace and love surround you. When something does come up that is troubling your mind, ask God for the answer. If your mind is clear, you might be surprised to receive the answer.

> Romans 10:17—So faith comes from hearing, that is, hearing the Good News about Christ.

> Revelations 4:1–2—Then, as I looked, I saw a door standing open in heaven, and the same

> voice I had heard before, spoke to me like a trumpet blast. The voice said, "Come up here, and I will show you what must happen after this." And instantly I was in the Spirit, and I saw a throne in heaven and someone sitting on it.
>
> Revelations 2:7—Anyone with ears to hear must listen to the Spirit and understand what he is saying to the churches. To everyone who is victorious I will give fruit from the tree of life in the paradise of God.

-The Spiritual Sense of Taste-

The Word of God feeds the hearts of those who seek after Him. Practice developing your power to actually taste the words of God (to experience or to perceive) in your heart while you are in meditation or prayer. Keep your favorite passages from the Bible with you or in your heart so the words of God are always there to feed your spirit.

When we would like someone to try a new food, we may say "Taste it, you will like it" or "You will never know if you like it until you try it." Scripture also uses this same approach for our sense of spiritual taste.

> Psalms 34:8—Taste and see that the Lord is good. Oh, the joys of those who take refuge in him!

Psalms 119:103—How sweet your words taste to me; they are sweeter than honey.

1 Peter 2:1–3—Therefore, rid yourselves of all malice and all deceit, hypocrisy, envy, and slander of every kind. Like newborn babies, crave pure spiritual milk, so that by it you may grow up in your salvation, now that you have tasted that the Lord is good.

Hebrews 6:4–5—For it is impossible to bring back to repentance those who were once enlightened—those who have experienced the good things of heaven and shared in the Holy Spirit, who have tasted the goodness of the Word of God and the power of the age to come.

-The Spiritual Sense of Touch-

Touch is the most personal and indispensable of the five senses. The sense of touch is the way infants learn about their environment and bond with others. People use their sense of touch to learn about the world around them, protect themselves, relate to others, and experience pleasure. The positive touch of others is necessary for an individual's healthy development. Despite the presence of all other life requirements, without this positive touch, infants will fail to develop normally. A child wants to be held and as soon as they are born, and as soon as they are able to crawl they want to touch everything within their reach.

> Matthew 20:34—Jesus felt sorry for them and touched their eyes. Instantly they could see! Then they followed him.

I find touch to be one of the most awesome of human experiences. For me, it embraces all of the other spiritual senses. Have you ever felt like you had the best conversation with yourself even when you did not say anything or you just all of a sudden had a revelation when you were not thinking about anything? Have you ever had a smile on your face and did not know why? Have you ever encountered the most eloquent silence? Have you ever experienced an awesome peace envelope you while you were listening to the rain or an inspiring song? Have you ever felt the beautiful smile of a child? Have you ever felt the touch of a beautiful flower or a beautiful sunset? These are the wonders of life that pull on our heart and touch us in the most profound way.

Some of life's most precious moments come to us as we feel the touch of God. Just imagine your life without even one of these experiences. Your life would be much less magical. These are the gifts of God's touch that endear us to Him and make life all the more worth living.

These awesome moments in time, no matter how small and short-lived are cherished forever as the most precious ones.

Mark 6:56—And wherever he went—into villages, towns or countryside—they placed the sick in the marketplaces. They begged him to let them touch even the edge of his cloak, and all who touched it were healed.

1 John 1:1—That which was from the beginning, which we have heard, which we have seen with our eyes, which we have looked at and our hands have touched—this we proclaim concerning the Word of life.

Genesis 3:3—but God did say, 'You must not eat fruit from the tree that is in the middle of the garden, and you must not touch it, or you will die.'

-The Spiritual Sense of Smell-

Your spiritual sense of smell is a powerful tool for conjuring up emotions and memories. When smelling a bunch of roses, you will experience the fragrance of roses. This would constitute a physical sense experience as there is a definite source of the fragrance. Yet, at the same time the fragrance enlightens your heart, which is a spiritual sense experience. At another time, you are sitting and having your morning coffee thinking about your workday and all of a sudden and with no apparent cause you sense a strong fragrance of roses. Later in the day the fragrance comes back again. You look around, but there is no apparent physical cause for the fragrance to be there. This would constitute a spiritual sense of smell. Has something like this ever happened to you? It has to me. It is important that we look at the spiritual side of all our senses and find how they can enlighten our lives.

> 2 Corinthians 2:14–15—But thank God! He has made us his captives and continues to lead us along in Christ's triumphal procession. Now he uses us to spread the knowledge of Christ everywhere, like a sweet perfume. Our lives are a Christ-like fragrance rising up to God. But this fragrance is perceived differently by those who are being saved and by those who are perishing.

> Psalms 45:8—Myrrh, aloes, and cassia perfume your robes. In ivory palaces the music of strings entertains you.

> Hosea 14:6—Its branches will spread out like beautiful olive trees, as fragrant as the cedars of Lebanon.

Created to Glorify God

Although God does not need anyone to make Him look good, believers should show, in all they say and do, how God has been good to them. We as believers have an awesome responsibility to bring God's glory into a world where self-pity, hatred, anger and revenge dominate the lives of so many people.

Many Christians think glorifying God simply means going to church and raising their hands in praise and worship. That is only part of it. If that is all we are doing to glorify God, we are making a mockery of God's goodness. The people in the church should already know how good God is. The people who need to see God's goodness are outside of the church.

> 1 Corinthians 10:31—So whether you eat or drink, or whatever you do, do it all for the glory of God.

What does it mean to glorify God? The Greek definition of the word 'glorify' means to magnify, to honor, to laud or to exalt. When we glorify God, we show by example how He is our Lord.

We glorify God by showing proper respect to all of His children. This means we are to show respect to everyone around us even if they are seemingly undeserving. A simple way to do this is to be a good neighbor. In the world we live in, most people do not even know who their neighbors are. The true nature of our heart is characterized by caring and giving.

> John 13:34–35—So now I (Jesus) am giving you a new commandment: Love each other. Just as I have loved you, you should love each

other. Your love for one another will prove to the world that you are my disciples.

Isaiah 42:5—God, the Lord, created the heavens and stretched them out. He created the earth and everything in it. He gives breath to everyone, life to everyone who walks the earth.

Each person living on the earth has been sent here to glorify God. Each person is here to serve God in a way no other person can. While for some people their purpose might be directly related to their job, for others it could simply be when they are of service to others.

Being in touch with God opens our spirit to imagination, intuition and insight. We become more energetically engaged in physical and spiritual unions. We were created in love, and there is no greater purpose in life than to share this love with others, especially with the lost. We need to ask ourselves the following questions:

- What makes my spirit come alive?
- When in my life do I feel a sense of God's awesome presence?
- In what ways do I feel led to serve others?
- When do I feel closest to God?
- How do I know when God is talking to me?
- What do I do that brings the peace of God into my life?

- What brings me true joy even in the worst of times?
- When do I experience the beauty in God's creation?
- When do I feel connected to the good in other people?

As serious Christians, we must be open and responsive to the world around us. In doing so, we must seek the divine within the world that invites, inspires, and reveals the spiritual nature of God. If we do not seek and search for God in the world around us, we will not find Him there.

Living as a Citizen of Heaven

Living as a citizen of heaven is not a secret waiting to be discovered. It comes from accepting Jesus' sacrifice on our behalf and by following the examples and teachings of His earthly ministry. Jesus came down from heaven for us and His life on earth demonstrates His heavenly citizenship. Jesus was in, but not of this world.

> John 6:38–40—For I have come down from heaven to do the will of God who sent me, not to do my own will. And this is the will of God, that I should not lose even one of all those he has given me, but that I should raise them up at the last day. For it is my Father's will that all who see his Son and believe in him should

have eternal life. I will raise them up at the last day."

John 17:5—Now, Father, bring me into the glory we shared before the world began.

John 17:8—For I have passed on to them the message you gave me. They accepted it and know that I came from you, and they believe you sent me.

John 8:23—Jesus continued, "You are from below; I am from above. You belong to this world; I do not.

Where is your citizenship? The citizenship of this world is only temporary. One day all of us will pass from this world and slip into the next. The most crucial question you should ask yourself is, "Where am I going to be?"

So how does one become a citizen of heaven? It starts by knowing you carry sin in your flesh and having a strong desire to be delivered from this sin. Sin cannot enter The Kingdom of God and because of sin, it leaves us on the outside looking in. When we accept the salvation offered by Jesus' death on the cross our sins are forgiven and we become heirs to His eternal Kingdom. Our name is written in the "Lambs Book of Life" and we become citizens of heaven.

The most powerful message I can give to you is that everything in this world pales in significance to eternity with God. What we need is a committed relationship with Jesus, separate from the nature of a fallen world and to live as though we are already living in our eternal home.

Paul struggled with the Commandments of "The Laws of Moses." He found that he was unable to keep all the commandments, leaving him condemned by the law. He knew that without the Spirit of Jesus residing within him, he would not be with Jesus when he moved from this world into the next.

Living as citizens of heaven is not abiding by an agenda or following a set of strict doctrines. Instead, it is characterized by the following:

- Seeking God with all your heart, soul, strength, and mind.

    Deuteronomy 4:29—But from there you will search again for the Lord your God. And if you search for him with all your heart and soul, you will find him.

- Knowing you are a new creation in Christ.

    2 Corinthians 5:17—This means that anyone who belongs to Christ has become a new person (creation). The old life is gone; a new life has begun!

- Transforming and renewing your mind.

    Romans 12:2—Don't copy the behavior and customs of this world, but let God transform you into a new person by changing the way you think. Then you will learn to know God's will for you, which is good and pleasing and perfect.

- Treating others as you would want to be treated.

    Philippians 2:3–4—Don't be selfish; don't try to impress others. Be humble, thinking of others as better than yourselves. Don't look out only for your own interests, but take an interest in others, too.

- Living your daily life in a relationship with Jesus.

    2 Peter 1:2–9—May God give you more and more grace and peace as you grow in your knowledge of God and Jesus our Lord. By his divine power, God has given us everything we need for living a godly life. We have received all of this by coming to know him, the one who called us to himself by means of his marvelous glory and excellence. And because of his glory and excellence, he has given us great and precious promises. These are the promises that enable you to share his divine nature

and escape the world's corruption caused by human desires. In view of all this, make every effort to respond to God's promises. Supplement your faith with a generous provision of moral excellence, and moral excellence with knowledge, and knowledge with self-control, and self-control with patient endurance, and patient endurance with godliness, and godliness with brotherly affection, and brotherly affection with love for everyone. The more you grow like this, the more productive and useful you will be in your knowledge of our Lord Jesus Christ.

- Sharing your faith with others.

  Matthew 5:14–16—You are the light of the world—like a city on a hilltop that cannot be hidden. No one lights a lamp and then puts it under a basket. Instead, a lamp is placed on a stand, where it gives light to everyone in the house. In the same way, let your good deeds shine out for all to see, so that everyone will praise your heavenly Father.

- Bearing fruit from your spiritual garden.

  Galatians 5:17—The sinful nature wants to do evil, which is just the opposite of what the Spirit wants. And the Spirit gives us desires that are the opposite of what the sinful nature desires. These two forces are constantly fighting each other, so you are not free to carry out your good intentions.

A Life Without God

I have heard many people say they are just fine without God. Do they not know the indescribable love, joy and peace that can only come from a relationship with Him? What about experiencing the awesome wonders of the spiritual world? What about having an inner peace, even in the worst of circumstances? What about knowing the meaning and purpose of your life? What about a true sense of purpose going from this life into the next?

I want you to know how important it is for you to have the revelational experiences of God in your life. God created you for His glory, and you will only find fulfillment and peace when you do what He designed you to do, be in a loving relationship with Him.

Most of us want equality and justice in the world. We want our lives to be like the stories we read as children, where our heroes win the battle, and the villains are brought to justice. Instead, we see the rich getting richer, the poor getting poorer, the moral decline of our youth and people in general becoming more apathetic.

The need for God has never been more evident than in our world today. Our absolute dependency on God should now be our greatest concern when we consider the evil growing around us.

Belief in God is the foundation from where all true knowledge comes. People cannot overcome the evil of this world if they do not have the knowledge of how and for what purpose they were created—to bring glory to their heavenly Father.

God's Holy Word, from cover to cover, states that the battle for our temporal soul centers upon who we choose to glorify, ourselves or God. Many scriptural texts describe the inevitable outcome of this battle of the ages. Those who glorify God will live with Him, those who glorify "self" will not.

Throughout the Christian life, the believer exercises faith in Jesus Christ and obedience to His Word. And from this faith and obedience is delivered from the bondage of sin.

> Romans 6:20–23—When you were slaves to sin, you were free from the obligation to do right. And what was the result? You are now ashamed of the things you used to do, things that end in eternal doom. But now you are free from the power of sin and have become slaves of God. Now you do those things that lead to holiness and result in eternal life. For the wages of sin is death, but the free gift of God is eternal life through Christ Jesus our Lord.

It was Jesus' love for you that caused Him to endure the cross. And He now invites you to come and have a personal relationship with Him, to be a new creation.

A spiritual journey into the world where God lives

Your spiritual state and eternal destiny are known by who you choose to serve. Are you waiting to overcome some specific sin in your life before you will accept Jesus, because you believe God will not accept you just as you are? Are you waiting for science to confirm God's existence or any other of the delay tactics Satan will use to keep you from having an eternal loving relationship with God? God has made it very clear as to how you can know Him, have your past, present, and future sins forgiven and have personal fellowship with Him right now. Jesus came so that each of us can live with Him in eternity.

Are you waiting for an invitation? Know that Jesus is waiting for you. He knows the intentions of your heart. If you would like to respond to His invitation, pray the following words with a sincere heart and Jesus will come and open your heart to the world where divine love, forgiveness, peace and joy reside.

> Jesus, I want to know you with all my heart. I ask forgiveness for all my sins. I want you to come into my heart and be Lord over my life. Thank you for dying on the cross for my sin so that I could be forgiven and forever live with you in Your eternal kingdom. I know you have the power to mold me into the person you created me to be. Thank you for loving me and giving me eternal life. I give my life over to you. Please guide and direct me along my spiritual journey. Amen.

What follows is an exciting lifelong journey of change and growth as you learn about your Creator. For those who would like to live the best life possible, the most memorable, powerful, enlightening, and spirit filled life—Jesus is the answer.

Find a Bible based church where you live. Study the Bible and learn to hear God's voice. Talk to Christians who know the reality of God. Ask Jesus to open your mind to an absolute assurance of His presence and He will answer that request. He will walk with you for the rest of your earthly life and will be there when you are ready to go home.

He Did Not Answer

(Author)
I asked God to taste His presence.
I did not taste His presence as I enjoyed dinner with my family.
I did not taste His presence as I relished my favorite desert.
I shouted to God, "I Want to Taste Your Presence!"
I did not taste His presence as I spread wild honey on my morning toast.
I asked God to sense His aroma.
I did not sense His aroma as I smelled Grandma's fresh-baked bread.
I did not sense His aroma as I smelled lilacs along a country road.
I shouted to God, "I Want to Sense Your Aroma!"

I did not sense His Aroma as I breathed in the fresh morning air.
I asked God to touch me.
I did not feel His touch as I felt the calmness of the ocean breeze.
I did not feel His touch as I brushed the butterfly away.
I shouted to God, "I Want You to Touch Me!"
I did not feel His touch as I held my son in my arms.
I asked God to see Him.
I did not see Him as I watched the sun rise over the horizon.
I did not see Him as I watched my daughters laugh and play.
I shouted to God, "I Want to See You!"
I did not see Him as I watched a rainbow appear after the rain.
I asked God to hear Him.
I did not hear Him as I was calmed by my favorite music.
I did not hear Him as I listened to the rain drops falling.
I shouted to God, "I Want to Hear You!"
I did not hear Him as the thunder roared during a rainstorm.
I cried out to God, "Where Are You!"
He did not answer.

The Apostles Peter, John, and James saw Jesus, Elijah and Moses in their spiritual bodies.

Luke 9:28–36

About eight days later Jesus took Peter, John, and James up on a mountain to pray. And as he was praying, the appearance of his face was transformed, and his clothes became dazzling white. Suddenly, two men, Moses and Elijah, appeared and began talking with Jesus. They were glorious to see. And they were speaking about his exodus from this world, which was about to be fulfilled in Jerusalem. Peter and the others had fallen asleep. When they woke up, they saw Jesus' glory and the two men standing with him. As Moses and Elijah were starting to leave, Peter, not even knowing what he was saying, blurted out, "Master, it's wonderful for us to be here! Let's make three shelters as memorials—one for you, one for Moses, and one for Elijah." But even as he was saying this, a cloud overshadowed them, and terror gripped them as the cloud covered them. Then a voice from the cloud said, "This is my Son, my Chosen One. Listen to him." When the voice finished, Jesus was there alone. They didn't tell anyone at that time what they had seen.

Chapter Five

A Spiritual Awakening

Ephesians 5:14
For it is light that makes everything visible. This is why it is said: "Awake, O sleeper, rise up from the dead, and Christ will give you light."

Awaken to the World Around You

We are greatly influenced by our surroundings in both a physical and spiritual way. For the spiritual part of us to come alive, we must seek those things that bring our spirit in tune with God. We must bring harmony between our spirit and God's Spirit to experience the extraordinary all around us. The term "awakening the spirit" includes times of spiritual enlightenment where God presents Himself through the beauty of His creation.

During the awakening process, there is a conscious awareness and recognition that something is different in our priorities, our sense of responsibility, and the way we react to both the positive and negative events happenings in the world around us. Experiences that were unknown reveal their meaning and our attitude toward the world we live in changes.

We feel a sense of calmness, clarity, and happiness. We see the extraordinary in things that went previously unnoticed and see beauty in the actual act of living each moment mindful of a loving God. We become aware of the spiritual world and the things a material world cannot provide. We rise up to find and claim our right to the joy and peace that God has made available to those who chose Him as Lord. We have chosen to overcome human limitations to reach the innate truth of our existence.

Awakening to the spiritual comes to those who strive to obtain it, seek until they find it, knock until it opens and question until answers are received. The desired result is a move towards positive thinking, loving servitude, exercising spiritual fruit, and the utilization of spiritual gifts.

With this awakening, spiritual fruit and spiritual gifts become a part of our life. Spiritual fruit comes naturally through the Holy Spirit, but spiritual gifts are only activated when we step out in righteous faith. When we step out in faith, we are stepping into the world of the supernatural.

For all those who cherish spiritual truth, beauty, and knowledge, waking the Spirit within you opens insights into the world beyond what the imagination could ever conceive of.

Bring to Life Your Spiritual Side

Jesus, at the cross, conquered death, hell, and sin. Dying on the cross was the foremost goal of Jesus—to overcome Man's spiritual death in the Garden of Eden by offering to renew the spirit of anyone who repents of their sin and accepts the salvation offered through His atoning blood sacrifice.

Our Sin-in-the-flesh nature has been passed down from Adam and is passed on to our children and their children. It is the sin of Adam that spiritually disconnected our spirit from God. It is the death and resurrection of Jesus Christ that reunites us with God.

> Ephesians 2:4-6—But God is so rich in mercy, and he loved us so much, that even though we were dead because of our sins, he gave us life when he raised Christ from the dead. (It is only by God's grace that you have been saved!) For he raised us from the dead along with Christ and seated us with him in the heavenly realms because we are united with Christ Jesus.

It is only through faith in Jesus as our redemptive Savior, that the punishment for sin can be removed and we can again have spiritual fellowship with God. So in

God's eyes, when we repent of our sin, thus believing in Jesus' death, burial, and resurrection, our sins are laid at the foot of the cross, and our spirit is renewer to its former state. This is the greatest news ever received anywhere at any time.

If you are not saved, do you have any idea what the power of the cross can do for you? Here is the revelation that our sins and the eternal punishment for them can be erased for all time. Thus, we are free from any condemnation because Jesus took our place and has already paid the fine in full. God, our heavenly Father remembers our sins no more.

> Hebrews 8:12—And I will forgive their wickedness, and I will never again remember their sins."

> John 1:29—The next day John saw Jesus coming toward him and said, "Look! The Lamb of God who takes away the sin of the world!

When our spirit has been renewed by the Spirit of God, we have the ability to transcend the natural world and see into the spiritual world. The outward portion of our being, our actions, now flows from the inward state of a renewed spirit connected to our heavenly Father.

To maintain our new spiritual awakening, we must listen to God's voice, spend time with Him in prayer and embed His Word in our heart. There is no shortcut;

there is no other way, and nobody can do it for you. It will not come by the laying on of hands, anointing oil, counseling, prophecy, or from any other person. It will only happen as you continually seek His presence. Also, books other than the Bible, such as Bible commentaries, Christian teachings, Christian novels, and early Christian texts can give you invaluable insights into your own spirituality and the spiritual world around you. But always understand, God's Word is the final authority.

Let Go of Attachments to a Material World

When we realize this earthly world is not our real home, we can concentrate more intently on our spiritual home. We are able to set our sights on heavenly things that have meaning and lasting value. We understand and realize that as believers we are to die to the things this world values: self-love, self-will, self-reliance, self-sufficiency, self-desires, self-pride, and selfish living. We are to ingrain God's love in us and then send it out into the world.

> 1 John 2:15–17—Do not love this world nor the things it offers you, for when you love the world, you do not have the love of the Father in you. For the world offers only a craving for physical pleasure, a craving for everything we see, and pride in our achievements and possessions. These are not from the Father, but are from this world. And this world is fading

away, along with everything that people crave. But anyone who does what pleases God will live forever.

God encourages all believers to grow in their relationship, commitment, and obedience to Him. We can all cultivate a greater awareness of the spiritual world and improve the quality of our life. It means not just having a conceptual or intellectual understanding of how we live on earth, but to internalize Christ's life by allowing Him to manifest through us into direct experience.

Having the power to be liberated from this world, "living in, but not of, the world," is a spiritual mindset that is attained only by living out the life of Christ.

Think of cause and effect, of reaping and sowing, because in response to any situation, internal or external, there are consequences both positive and negative. Every time we choose a positive reaction, our spirit grows and we become more and more liberated from our ties to this world. Every time we choose a negative response we become more and more tethered to a dying world.

> Galatians 6:8—Those who live only to satisfy their own sinful nature will harvest decay and death from that sinful nature, but those who live to please the Spirit will harvest everlasting life from the Spirit.

> Hosea 10:12—I said, 'Plant the good seeds of righteousness, and you will harvest a crop

of love. Plow up the hard ground of your hearts, for now is the time to seek the LORD that he may come and shower righteousness upon you.'

James 3:17–18—But the wisdom from above is first of all pure. It is also peace loving, gentle at all times, and willing to yield to others. It is full of mercy and the fruit of good deeds. It shows no favoritism and is always sincere. And those who are peacemakers will plant seeds of peace and reap a harvest of righteousness.

So where do we go from here?

In many respects, the answer is as unique as we are. The way each of us experience God will be somewhat different, depending on how diligently we seek Him and how faithfully we apply His written Word to our lives.

In Paul's letter to the Colossians, we find him telling his readers what he prayed for on their behalf. By studying this passage, we can learn not only what Paul desired for the Colossians, but also what God desires for us. This scripture is a covenant prayer addressed to God, that if we do our part He will do His part. It is an affirmation of our desire and willingness to seek after spiritual growth and an agreement with God that He will fulfill this desire.

A Spiritual Awakening

I find this scripture to be very powerful and helpful when I need to be reminded of just how great God is and what He expects from me.

> Colossians 1:9–19—So we have not stopped praying for you since we first heard about you. We ask God to give you complete knowledge of his will and to give you spiritual wisdom and understanding. Then the way you live will always honor and please the Lord, and your lives will produce every kind of good fruit. All the while, you will grow as you learn to know God better and better. We also pray that you will be strengthened with all his glorious power so you will have all the endurance and patience you need. May you be filled with joy, always thanking the Father. He has enabled you to share in the inheritance that belongs to his people, who live in the light. For he has rescued us from the kingdom of darkness and transferred us into the Kingdom of his dear Son, who purchased our freedom and forgave our sins. Christ is the visible image of the invisible God. He existed before anything was created and is supreme over all creation, for through him God created everything in the heavenly realms and on earth. He made the things we can see and the things we can't see—such as thrones, kingdoms, rulers, and authorities in the unseen world. Everything

was created through him and for him. He existed before anything else, and he holds all creation together. Christ is also the head of the church, which is his body. He is the beginning, supreme over all who rise from the dead. So he is first in everything. For God in all his fullness was pleased to live in Christ.

A Broken Connection

During the creation process, our spirit was created in the image of God, which emanated from His Spirit and gave us life.

> Genesis 2:7—Then the LORD God formed the man from the dust of the ground. He breathed the breath of life into the man's nostrils, and the man became a living person.

The breath of life was the Spirit of God making Man a living physical being with a spirit and soul. Man's spirit connected him to God, allowing them to commune with one another. Man was also given free will—the power to choose to obey God, or not.

Genesis chapter three tells us that our spirit lost its connection with God because of disobedience. When our spiritual link to God was severed, our eyes were opened to the knowledge of good and evil. Without this spiritual link to God, Man lost his privileged status, and became lost in a self-centered world.

The first thing Adam and Eve did after they had disobeyed God was to sew fig leaves around themselves to hide their nakedness. Afterward, when they heard God calling, they hid from Him among the trees of the Garden. God covered their nakedness with animal skins because they were now alone and felt shame; from that point on a self-centered sin nature was to be a part of Man's inheritance.

Our soul which is the source of our natural instincts and drives, without a spiritual connection to God will tend to choose what we believe is just and right for ourselves without considering how our actions may affect others.

Until we are restored to our original spiritual state we are bound to a self-centered nature, where it is possible for our conscience to be seared to the level of total self-gratification. This is seen in people who lack any moral code of ethics.

> 1 Timothy 4:1–2—Now the Holy Spirit tells us clearly that in the last times some will turn away from the true faith; they will follow deceptive spirits and teachings that come from demons. These people are hypocrites and liars, and their consciences are dead.

Walking Along the Path Jesus Set for Us

Just before Jesus' death on the cross, He promised His disciples that God would send an Advocate after

He returned to heaven. The Advocate, Jesus promised is God's Holy Spirit.

> John 14:26—But when the Father sends the Advocate as my representative—that is, the Holy Spirit—he will teach you everything and will remind you of everything I have told you.

> John 14:15-17—"If you love me, obey my commandments. And I will ask the Father, and he will give you another Advocate, who will never leave you. He is the Holy Spirit, who leads into all truth. The world cannot receive him, because it isn't looking for him and doesn't recognize him. But you know him (Christ), because he lives with you now and later will be in you.

When we walk along the path Jesus set for us, our eyes open to a new spiritual reality. The natural Man and his ideas begin to fade away, and the Holy Spirit empowers us and changes us. Jesus becomes preeminent in our lives as we open our spirit and heart to His Spirit of Truth.

When we walk in the path God set for us, we enter a world where the spiritual side of life becomes known. It is a transformation of physical consciousness to spiritual consciousness; of being self-centered to being God-centered. For most of us it is not an event, but is a process we undergo in our search for God. Even those rare people who experience a sudden, dramatic and seemingly instant spiritual awakening will still go through a process in which their new state of consciousness gradually flows into them and transforms everything they do as God becomes preeminent in their life.

The initiation of the spiritual awakening process comes to us by God's grace. Once you awaken to God's presence, you know it firsthand. It is no longer just something someone else has told you about. The spiritual world has become a reality.

People who have experienced this awakening process realize that what this world has to offer is a weak reflection of what God has to offer. They finally reach the realization there is a sacred dimension of reality we can enter to discern the spiritual side of life.

If we follow the path Jesus set for us, we will have all we need to be the person God wants us to be. The Bible tells us who God is, what He is like, and how to live within His will. In addition to the Bible, God gives us His Holy Spirit to guide and direct us along our spiritual journey.

Awaken Your Spirit to the Beautiful

I know that when my spirit is in tune with God's Spirit, I can reach out in a moment of time and find myself in the presence of God.

> Hilary Cooper: Life is not measured by the number of breaths we take, but by the moments that take our breath away. http://forum.quoteland.com/eve/forums/

> 1 Chronicles 16:29—Give to the Lord the glory he deserves! Bring your offering and come into his presence. Worship the Lord in all his holy splendor.

I am aware that these momentary interventions by divine grace are some of the most remarkable and beautiful events that have occurred in my lifetime. It happens with an extraordinary combination of circumstances that permits me to let completely go of self and to allow an intervention of a spiritual awakening. This may come in a child's smile, a lovely flower, a beautiful sunset, or anything that brings a divine intervention of God in my life.

We need to understand that God is the source of all divine encounters. The self-centered choices we make are a parting from God that asserts itself over what we know to be right and just. It is only the moment by moment spiritual consciousness of the divine that allows us to see beyond self and at times, to realize we are in God's presence.

Being aware of God's presence is not easy sometimes because of the unyielding compulsion of "self" getting in the way. It is utterly impossible to commune with God when our world revolves around our self-centered nature.

Being connected to the beauty God brings to us allows us to have more and more moments with Him.

The Essence of Spiritual Beauty

When we express our being in the dimension of beauty, with love and with the talents and gifts God has given us, we are communicating the divine beauty of God's Spirit to the outside world.

When we hear the word beautiful, we invariably think of that place where the extraordinary lives: beautiful art, beautiful flowers, beautiful sunsets, beautiful rainbows, beautiful music, and beautiful people.

Without realizing it, each one of us is visited every day by God's beauty we do not take the time to see. We seem to always be in a hurry to get somewhere and to satisfy our longing for things we do not need. When we talk with people, it is no surprise that beauty is rarely mentioned. We hear about the self, their day, how they feel, how they were not able to do this or that, or what someone has done to them. A world without God's beauty would be unimaginable.

It is the subtle touch of beauty in our world that stirs our soul and helps us to get through the troubled times. How much greater life's experiences would be if we would just take the time to stop and admire the beautiful things that cross our path each day.

In Greek, the word for beauty *kilos* means to be called to. When we experience beauty, we are called or drawn to it. Beauty stirs passion in our souls when we let it envelop our spirit and feel the warmth and wonder of its embrace. The sense of beauty connects us to a world beyond our own. It awakens our soul and takes us to a world outside of self.

Have you ever heard someone say that they never tire of driving along the same beautiful patch of road or how they love to take a walk on a beautiful spring day? It is the drawing of their soul to be in touch with their Creator. What is the first thing you try to do when you are holding a baby or playing with a young child? You try to make them smile and laugh. If you watch people when they do this you will see them smiling and at times acting more like the child they are trying to captivate. They are waking the beauty of their soul.

Beauty does not need to be a chance occurrence in our everyday lives; it unveils itself to all who seek it. In its most profound sense, beauty is a spiritual awareness that connects us to our Creator and brings us into His presence. Beauty only visits us for moments in time, yet these encounters leave us with a profound sense of spiritual well-being. We intuitively know the very essence of a beautiful moment is real.

Beauty of the Inner Self

All of God's children should create, support, and encourage the growth of beauty around them by their actions and deeds. Their spiritual beauty brings out the beauty in others.

A Spiritual Awakening

There are many good looking people on the outside, but their hearts are ugly on the inside and therefore, their outward beauty is only a superficial form of who they really are. On the other hand, there are many people who are not so good looking on the outside, but on the inside there is a loving, kind and gentle spirit; and when these attributes shine through it makes them very beautiful. It is our inner beauty that shows our true worth as a child of God.

Inner beauty comes when we live according to God's ordinances. It shows itself in the way we treat others and even in the way we treat ourselves. Real beauty is found in the willingness to put our self aside.

> James 1:19–25—Understand this, my dear brothers and sisters: You must all be quick to listen, slow to speak, and slow to get angry. Human anger does not produce the righteousness God desires. So get rid of all the filth and evil in your lives, and humbly accept the Word God has planted in your hearts, for it has the power to save your souls. But don't just listen to God's Word. You must do what it says otherwise you are only fooling yourselves. For if you listen to the Word and don't obey it is like glancing at your face in a mirror. You see yourself, walk away, and forget what you look like. But if you look carefully into the perfect law that sets you free, and if you

do what it says and don't forget what you heard, then God will bless you for doing it.

My grandmother would always tell me, "beauty is as beauty does" when she was counseling me about my behavior. Her mother used this saying, and I have continued the tradition in my family. There is a reason this saying has been around for eons; it is correct about appearances being misleading.

Inner beauty is not about what we see when we look at someone, but more about what we sense or feel. We will feel inspired, warm, calm, and connected to the best in ourselves when in the presence of a beautiful spirit. Seek out these people in your life.

Gossip is one of the greatest destroyers of inner beauty; it comes from a self-centered need to lift one's self up by putting others down. This type of conversation only reinforces our obsession to be more than we are. Negative comments come from a self-centered nature; positive comments come from an inner beauty that inspires those around us.

> Ephesians 4:29—Don't use foul or abusive language. Let everything you say be good and helpful, so that your words will be an encouragement to those who hear them.

> Leviticus 19:16—Do not spread slanderous gossip among your people. Do not stand idly

by when your neighbor's life is threatened. I am the LORD.

Exodus 20:16—You must not testify falsely against your neighbor.

An anonymous poem

There is enough bad in the best of us
and enough good in the worst of us,
so that it should hardly behoove any of us
to talk about the rest of us.

Take the time to compliment the inner beauty of your friends, family, coworkers, acquaintances, and even strangers. Drawing attention to their inner beauty will encourage them to sow beautiful seeds. Surround yourself with people who make appreciating inner beauty a top priority and allow it to become prominent in your life.

Physical beauty is a superficial form and has nothing to do with the beauty that comes from the inside. Inner beauty inspires you, uplifts your spirit and draws you to it. How long could you be around a good looking heartless and insensitive person? Not long. Being around a person that is not beautiful on the inside can quickly strip joy, happiness and contentment from your life.

Beauty on the Outside Fades Away

Many people hold on to what they can physically understand and touch, the material world. They rarely look for the beauty on the inside; how a seed grows, how a flower blossom or how creation unfolds and continues.

We need to understand that physical beauty is temporary and passing, but spiritual beauty is everlasting. People see a beautiful person on the outside, and their affection is immediately drawn to them. Their notion of beauty is limited to something that is skin deep. So they enter into a relationship with the object of their affection and it fails. They have been deceived by outward appearances.

> Romans 9:20–21—No, don't say that. Who are you, a mere human being, to argue with God? Should the thing that was created say to the one who created it, "Why have you made me like this?" When a potter makes jars out of clay, doesn't he have a right to use the same lump of clay to make one jar for decoration and another to throw garbage into?

Everywhere we look we are faced with the world's view of beauty. We see it when we turn on our television or flip through our favorite magazine. Beauty is often shown as being tall and skinny, with perfect makeup, clothing, and jewelry. Corporations would have us believe that a person's self-worth comes from how beautiful they look on the outside. People who are superficial take this to the extreme and image becomes more important than character.

> A Quote by Leo Tolstoy "The Kreutzer Sonata (p. 78) "It is amazing how complete is the delusion that beauty is goodness."

God made us to see the beauty in who we are as His children and to make the most out of what he has blessed us with. His Word tells us that outward adornment is not real beauty, but beauty that comes from the inside is of great worth.

> 1 Peter 3:3–4—Don't be concerned about the outward beauty of fancy hairstyles, expensive jewelry, or beautiful clothes. You should clothe yourselves instead with the beauty that comes from within, the unfading beauty of a gentle and quiet spirit, which is so precious to God.

This scripture is saying that real beauty comes from our spiritual nature; it is a gift from our Creator. The more beautiful our spirit, the more of God's beauty we pass to the outside world.

Opening the Spiritual World

"The Heavens" or "Heavenly Places/Realms" are names used in the Bible to describe the spiritual world. Seeing the spiritual world is not complex or difficult. It is so simple we often miss the simplicity of it, and yet because of the lack of belief or fear, few seek it.

Seeing the spiritual world will become a natural occurrence when you dedicate your life to the teachings of Jesus Christ. Jesus came to teach us to love and to forgive unconditionally and universally. The life of Jesus is the key to seeing past the physical world and into the spiritual world.

> Ephesians 1:3–4—All praise to God, the Father of our Lord Jesus Christ, who has blessed us with every spiritual blessing in the heavenly realms because we are united with Christ. Even before he made the world, God loved us and chose us in Christ to be holy and without fault in his eyes.
>
> Ephesians 2:6—For he raised us from the dead along with Christ and seated us with him in the heavenly realms because we are united with Christ Jesus.

I have found eight things that help open the spiritual world. I hope they will be of help to you.

A Spiritual Awakening

1. A Strong Desire (Motive and Intent).

You must first have a strong desire to see the spiritual world. You must be steadfast in your resolve and consciously seek it.

> Psalms 37:4—Take delight in the Lord, and he will give you your heart's desires.

2. Intense Prayer.

Through daily prayer, ask God for the gift of spiritual discernment. Pray continually and intently for your spiritual eyes to open. Never give up looking for it to happen. The Bible tells us that the person who has the Spirit of God indwelling has the ability to see the spiritual world, but it is up to us to open our eyes. God's divine plan is that all His children would know the spiritual world. When He tells us to talk to Him and to ask, He is trying to involve us in His blessing. He wants us to experience the fullness of our inheritance that comes through His Son.

> 2 Corinthians 4:4—Satan, who is the god of this world, has blinded the minds of those who don't believe. They are unable to see the glorious light of the Good News. They don't understand this message about the glory of Christ, who is the exact likeness of God.

> John 12:46—I have come as a light to shine in this dark world, so that all who put their trust in me will no longer remain in the dark.

3. Meditation.

Meditating on God's Word while quieting your mind will assist you in making a connection to the spiritual world. During quiet meditation visualize what you think seeing the spiritual world will be like.

> Psalms 63:6—I lie awake thinking of you, meditating on you through the night.

> 1 Timothy 4:15—Give your complete attention to these matters. Throw yourself into your tasks so that everyone will see your progress. Keep a close watch on how you live and on your teaching. Stay true to what is right for the sake of your own salvation and the salvation of those who hear you.

4. Stop, Look, and Listen.

Be in tune (aware) of the spiritual things going on around you. Always be aware of both your physical senses and your spiritual senses. God and His angels are constantly working in the lives of believers. Stop, look and listen for spiritual signs, symbols and messages throughout your day and take note of exactly how and when they happen.

These events may come in your dreams, in a song, in events that strike you as coincidental, a strong feeling of contentment and peace, or anything that lifts your spirit beyond the ordinary.

5. Do Everything with Praise and Thanksgiving.

Find spiritual music that lifts your spirit beyond this world then streach out your arms in praise to a loving Father.

Never forget to thank God whenever He blesses you with an unexpected spiritual experience.

> Matthew 11:25—At that time Jesus prayed this prayer: "O Father, Lord of heaven and earth, thank you for hiding these things from those who think themselves wise and clever, and for revealing them to the childlike.

6. Walk in t.he Spirit.

Walking in the Spirit is to let flow from of your heart the virtues of love, joy, peace, forbearance, kindness, goodness, faithfulness, gentleness, and self-control. These virtues should be on constant display.

> Romans 8:1–2—So now there is no condemnation for those who belong to Christ Jesus.

And because you belong to him, the power of the life-giving Spirit has freed you from the power of sin that leads to death.

7. Glorify God in everything you say and do.

Glorifying God is always giving Him the honor He deserves as your Lord and Savior. You need to thank Him for the joy, hope, peace, contentment, and the blessings He gives to you each day.

> Psalms 150:1–6—Praise God in his sanctuary; praise him in his mighty heaven! Praise him for his mighty works; praise his unequaled greatness! Praise him with a blast of the ram's horn; praise him with the lyre and harp! Praise him with the tambourine and dancing; praise him with strings and flutes! Praise him with a clash of cymbals; praise him with loud clanging cymbals. Let everything that breathes sing praises to the Lord!

8. Daily worship.

Jesus makes it quite clear that worship is about far more than just going to church. In fact, in the context of the following scripture, he's not talking about the church at all when he defines true worship. He's talking about a lifestyle. He's talking about turning our lives over to

God, and being eager to pursue the truth by studying His Word.

> John 4:23–24—But the time is coming—indeed, it's here now—when true worshipers will worship the Father in spirit and in truth. The Father is looking for those who will worship him that way. For God is Spirit, so those who worship him must worship in spirit and in truth."

Without realizing it, each one of us is visited each day by the spirit of beauty we do not take the time to see.

Psalm 50:2
From Mount Zion, the perfection of beauty, God shines in glorious radiance.

Chapter Six

Cultivating Spiritual Fruit

John 15:5
"Yes, I am the vine; you are the branches. Those who remain in me, and I in them, will produce much fruit. For apart from me (Jesus) you can do nothing.

The more seeds of Love you sow, the more love grows in your heart and the hearts of others.

Sending the Fruit of God's Love out into the World

Galatians 5:22–23—But the Holy Spirit produces this kind of fruit in our lives: love, joy, peace, patience, kindness, goodness, faithfulness, gentleness, and self-control. There is no law against these things!

Cultivating Spiritual Fruit

Fruit of the Spirit (fruit that comes from the Spirit of God within you) is not inherent in the physical world; it comes from and is a part of the spiritual world. The spreading of Spiritual Fruit into the natural world is perceived and experienced through an individual's spirit. Fruit of the Spirit cannot be taught or bought and can only come to the surface by a spiritual response to God's grace. One of the great things about spiritual fruit is when you give it away you receive some in return.

> Nehemiah 8:10—Nehemiah said, "Go and enjoy choice food and sweet drinks, and send some to those who have nothing prepared. This day is holy to our Lord. Do not grieve, for the joy of the LORD is your strength."

> 2 Corinthians 6:6—We prove ourselves by our purity, our understanding, our patience, our kindness, by the Holy Spirit within us, and by our sincere love.

God desires that we always grow in faith. This involves recognizing and demonstrating the Fruit of the Spirit to all of God's creation. We, as God's children need to recognize and clearly understand that:

- Fruit of the Spirit comes from God and is for all His children.
- Bearing fruit can only come from the spiritual part of our true self.

- The demonstration of our spiritual fruit is God manifesting His love through us.
- Spiritual fruit comes from God and expresses itself through His children.
- The manifestation of each person's spiritual fruit benefits everyone.
- Spiritual fruit brings enlightenment and healing to all.
- Spiritual fruit is born in love and results in love for all of God's creation.
- Spiritual fruit is kind and gentle not coercive or selfish.
- Spiritual fruit does not flatter the self, but supports the true essence of our nature.
- Spiritual fruit brings fun, adventure, truth, and light into our earthly journey.

Divine Love is the Seed from which All Other Spiritual Fruit Blossoms

When we talk about God's love, we are talking about a Divine Love—a Holy Spirit Love. Throughout the Bible, it is taught that the Love of God is unconditional and uncompromised. It is to be shown to everyone and everything.

In God's Word, more emphasis is placed on the fruit defined as "Love" than any other, because of its major importance to God. As Jesus loves us and forgives us of our sin, we are to love and forgive others of their sin against us. Let God's Holy Spirit manifest His love in you and through you. God wants you to give all the love you can and never give up trying to give more. Love is a never ending commodity. You will find that the more love you give away, the more love returns to you. It really works!

The lives of believers are challenging, yet rewarding when they arrive at their heavenly home. A faithful believer pouring out God's love into the world is able to accomplish great things.

> Matthew 22:36-40—"Teacher, which is the most important commandment in the law of Moses?" Jesus replied, "'you must love the Lord your God with all your heart, all your soul, and all your mind.' This is the first and greatest commandment. A second is equally important: 'Love your neighbor as yourself.' The entire law and all the demands of the prophets are based on these two commandments."

Love's Supreme Importance

Paul in his letter to the Corinthians reveals love's supreme importance in life. Paul directly compares love to faith, prophecy, sacrifice, knowledge and all the spiritual gifts.

> 1 Corinthians 13:1-8—If I could speak all the languages of earth and of angels, but didn't love others, I would only be a noisy gong or a

clanging cymbal. If I had the gift of prophecy, and if I understood all of God's secret plans and possessed all knowledge, and if I had such faith that I could move mountains, but didn't love others, I would be nothing. If I gave everything I have to the poor and even sacrificed my body, I could boast about it; but if I didn't love others, I would have gained nothing. Love is patient and kind. Love is not jealous or boastful or proud or rude. It does not demand its own way. It is not irritable, and it keeps no record of being wronged. It does not rejoice about injustice, but rejoices whenever the truth wins out. Love never gives up, never loses faith, is always hopeful, and endures through every circumstance. Prophecy and speaking in unknown languages and special knowledge will become useless. But love will last forever!

Spiritual fruit and spiritual gifts can only flourish when activated by love; love being the most powerful energy in the spiritual world.

> 1 Corinthians 14:1—Let love be your highest goal! But you should also desire the special abilities the Spirit gives—especially the ability to prophesy.

When we look at the Fruit of the Spirit beginning in Galatians 5:22, it says "the Fruit of the Spirit is love." I see the fruits that follow as love's virtues: "joy, peace, kindness, goodness, faithfulness, gentleness, and self-control."

It is easy to understand that we are to put on the virtues of love when we read Paul's letter to the Colossians. Notice that love is the perfect unity of all virtues.

> Colossians 3:12–14—Since God chose you to be the holy people he loves, you must clothe yourselves with tenderhearted mercy, kindness, humility, gentleness, and patience. Make allowance for each other's faults, and forgive anyone who offends you. Remember, the Lord forgave you, so you must forgive others. Above all, clothe yourselves with love, which binds us all together in perfect harmony.

As Christians, we need to understand that "to walk in love" is to honor God by cultivating the Fruit of the Spirit.

> 2 John 1:6—Love means doing what God has commanded us, and he has commanded us to love one another, just as you heard from the beginning.

> Ephesians 5:2—Live a life filled with love, following the example of Christ. He loved

us and offered himself as a sacrifice for us, a pleasing aroma to God.

1 Corinthians 13:13—Three things will last forever—faith, hope, and love—and the greatest of these is love.

Ephesians 3:17-19—So that Christ may dwell in your hearts through faith. And I pray that you, being rooted and established in love, may have power, together with all the Lord's holy people, to grasp how wide and long and high and deep is the love of Christ, and to know this love that surpasses knowledge—that you may be filled to the measure of all the fullness of God

1 John 4:16-17—Then Christ will make his home in your hearts as you trust in him. Your roots will grow down into God's love and keep you strong. And may you have the power to understand, as all God's people should, how wide, how long, how high, and how deep his love is. May you experience the love of Christ, though it is too great to understand fully. Then you will be made complete with all the fullness of life and power that comes from God.

God's Love is Supernatural

We spend so much time waiting to be loved, hoping love will find us, yearning and searching for that special love and feeling empty and lost without it. We have a deep need for someone to show us love and make us feel wanted. Unfortunately, that is not always how life works.

One of the reasons we do not receive the love we desire is that we have little love to give. Keeping God's love inside us is paramount to loving ourselves and others. This is the only dependable way to create an atmosphere where true love can thrive. When we expect to fill the void of love from a source outside of ourselves, we can end up hurt and feeling rejected. To be able to love ourselves and others, we must first have the love of God in our heart and mind.

> Mother Teresa: "The hunger for love is much more difficult to remove than the hunger for bread."

Gotta Love "Me"

When I first became aware that I needed to love myself, I realized I did not know where to begin. It was a surprise to me as I would have thought I would be an expert on love and relationships by the age of thirty. After all, I had been through what I thought were loving relationships. I soon realized my search was not for someone I could love, but I was looking for someone that could love me to fill an emptiness I had inside. I realized I had failed miserably in my early courtships because I had insufficient love for the person called "me." I had little love to give so I received little in return.

I suffered from low self-esteem and found it difficult to find even a little love for myself. My mind was so ingrained with self-sabotaging thoughts for the longest time that loving me was not something I considered.

However, I knew that if I were ever to have a long term loving relationship I would have to make a conscious effort to change. I realized that when you do not have love for yourself, you are basically telling the universe you are unworthy and undeserving of love.

Everyone has a calling from God. I had heard my call, but rejected His plea. I knew it would be in my best interest to answer this call, but I was sure I could handle it on my own. I would just work on my personal growth and development. Well, that did not work. I knew I needed to take care of myself physically, mentally and emotionally, but my poorly conceived lifestyle always won out. No matter what I did to fill the void inside of me, I still felt empty and was unable to maintain a meaningful relationship. When I hit rock bottom, my brain finally realized I was in need of help.

One night I seriously answered God's call and my life began to change. He told me all about the unconditional love He had just for me and that I was to make His love a part of my life. I cannot begin to tell you of the awesome experiences He had in store for me. I now understood what it means to be truly loved. The great thing about this love is that it is available to anyone who seeks it.

All of us are in need of a love greater than any love found in this world. God will give you the love and spiritual capability to rise above whatever conditions and obstacles obstruct your path as long as you keep your eyes on Him. Get to know the person God made; you will be pleasantly surprised.

So if you have decided to open your heart to God's unconditional love, but are not sure how to go about doing it, the following is a list of affirmations that can be of great help. This list of life-changing affirmations can give you the freedom to have a life filled with the best God has to offer. If these statements have meaning for you, practice any or all of them until they become a natural part of your life.

- I will not spend my life in the past.
- I will make my life better, one day at a time.
- I will not criticize myself or accept criticism from others.
- I will be tolerant and patient with myself.
- I will give my worries over to God.
- I will have confidence in all that I do.
- I will be truthful about my feelings.
- I will spend time with God.
- I will express my appreciation for the life God has given me.
- I will take time to feed my mind, body and spirit.
- I will take the time to see and feel the beauty of God's creation.
- I will take the time to see the beauty in others.

- I will show love towards all of God's creation.
- I will show love to the person God created—Me!

Psalms 34:5–7—Those who look to him for help will be radiant with joy; no shadow of shame will darken their faces. In my desperation I prayed, and the Lord listened; he saved me from all my troubles. For the angel of the Lord is a guard; he surrounds and defends all who fear him.

Matthew 6:34—"So don't worry about tomorrow, for tomorrow will bring its own worries. Today's trouble is enough for today.

Do not just blindly follow anyone. Learn to make your own life choices by following God's Word and the moral compass He put in your heart.

Caring for Your Spirit

If you take care of your mind and body, but neglect your spirit, you will lack the ability to experience fully the awesome moments of life God has planned for you. Taking care of your spirit helps when the stresses and challenges of everyday life try to take you down.

If you love yourself, you will invest both in your personal and spiritual growth. You will endeavor to be the best that you can be and you will continually strive to bring out the best in others.

Loving yourself lifts both your confidence and your self-esteem. When you suffer from low self-esteem, it is impossible to reach out and become the loving person God knows you to be.

When you make a decision to love yourself, you are really saying that you want to accept who you are right now and start on a quest to become the person you know yourself to be. You accept that you are responsible for both the choices you make and the outcomes those choices produce.

You cannot sit around waiting for others to accept who you are. You are the only you, you have—make it the best you that you can be.

Love Your Enemy?

Who are these people that dislike you and why should you love them? Maybe it is someone who has picked on you, called you names, or disrespected you in some manner that caused you to hold on to anger, hurt, or disappointment. Maybe it is a family member that you have had a fight with recently or in the past, someone who did something terrible to someone you know, or someone who just irritates you to no end. How do you handle it? What does God mean when He tells you to love these people?

Jesus taught "love your neighbor," which can be a difficult thing in itself, but to "love your enemies" has to be one of the greatest challenges in life. How can you love someone who engenders hatred, and you feel is your enemy. Do you have to show loving feelings toward those who despise you or are persecuting you? The answer is a resounding "No!" When God tells you to love your enemies, He is not talking about feelings. He is telling you to choose to care for your enemies if they are truly in need, because of who they are—His children.

> Luke 6:27—But to you who are willing to listen, I say, love your enemies! Do good to those who hate you.

> Matthew 5:43–48—"You have heard the law that says, 'Love your neighbor' and hate your enemy. But I say, love your enemies! Pray for those who persecute you! In that way, you will be acting as true children of your Father in heaven. For he gives his sunlight to both the evil and the good, and he sends rain on the just and the unjust alike. If you love only those who love you, what reward is there for that? Even corrupt tax collectors do that much. If you are kind only to your friends, how are you different from anyone else? Even pagans do that. But you are to be perfect, even as your Father in heaven is perfect.

The animosity we feel towards those who offend us can build up inside and eventually cause us to take destructive actions to satisfy our need for revenge. This is in direct conflict with the commandment "to love your enemies." This does not mean we have to like our enemy or should not protect ourselves if we are assaulted in some fashion.

What it does mean is to let go of the anger and hatred that revenge stirs inside of us. God wants us to turn these destructive emotions over to Him because of the harm they cause to our physical, emotional and spiritual well-being. God loves us and wants us to have the best life possible.

> John 13:34–35—So now I (Jesus) am giving you a new commandment: Love each other. Just as I have loved you, you should love each other. Your love for one another will prove to the world that you are my disciples."

All biblical laws are based on and dependent on our love for God, love for ourselves and love for our neighbors.

> 1 Timothy 1:5—The purpose of my instruction is that all believers would be filled with love that comes from a pure heart, a clear conscience, and genuine faith.
>
> Ephesians 4:21–25—Through the filling of God's Holy Spirit, we are able to fellowship with Jesus and to follow in His footsteps, we are able to follow our higher nature and stop making provision for our lower or sinful

nature. Since you have heard about Jesus and have learned the truth that comes from him, throw off your old sinful nature and your former way of life, which is corrupted by lust and deception. Instead, let the Spirit renew your thoughts and attitudes. Put on your new nature, created to be like God—truly righteous and holy. So stop telling lies. Let us tell our neighbors the truth, for we are all parts of the same body.

In the above scripture we can see that our sin nature hinders God's command to love one another and to worship with one another. We need the life-changing power of Jesus Christ in us to bring our life into accordance with His will.

Harvesting from the Tree of Love
Fruit produced through the indwelling of the Holy Spirit

-Joy-

Joy is usually associated with happiness. Look in any dictionary and you will see joy and happiness defined as closely related terms. However, the Bible interprets joy in a very different way. Like love, God-given joy is not the product of the natural world.

Scripture speaks much more about being joyful than of being happy. Happiness is an emotion that depends

on something good happening. God wants us to experience an immeasurable and indescribable kind of happiness that does not require anything good to happen. God's Joy" comes to us when we have a relationship with His Son—Jesus Christ.

> John 15:10–11—When you obey my commandments, you remain in my love, just as I obey my Father's commandments and remain in his love. I have told you these things so that you will be filled with my joy. Yes, your joy will overflow!

> Psalms 35:27—But give great joy to those who came to my defense. Let them continually say, "Great is the LORD, who delights in blessing his servant with peace!"

If you were all alone in the world with no one to be with, to talk to, to share your life with, to share intimate moments with, to laugh with, to hold, to love you, to encourage you, what would your life be like? It is the joy of others and the joy found in serving a loving God that allows us to find our greatest fulfillment in life. Seeing the joy in each other brightens our own spirit and enhances the beauty in the world around us.

> Ecclesiastes 3:4—A time to cry and a time to laugh. A time to grieve and a time to dance.

If you are filled with God's love, joy follows. Joy is fully attainable throughout your life. Joy comes just by knowing you are in the hands of the Master.

I stopped by the woods on my way home from the store to watch three fawns playing by the side of the road. Soon there were several cars of people watching. The fawns were jumping around, running into each other, and just having a good time. My only thought was how wonderful the joy God has given to His creation. God brings these kinds of joy into all of our lives if only we take the time to see them.

-Peace-

The world we see outside of ourselves is simply a mental reflection of the world we have shaped and modeled within ourselves. The level of stress or peace we experience in our lives is in direct correlation to the level of stress or peace we have within ourselves. The more peace we have in our inner world, the more peace we will experience and extend to the outer world. Whereas, the more stress in our inner world, the more stress we will experience and extend into the outer world. As we change our thoughts and attitudes from the inside we change our perceptions of the world and the way we react and participate in it.

> James 3:18—Now may the Lord of peace himself give you his peace at all times and in every situation. The Lord be with you all.

The inner spiritual (divine) peace that comes to those who belong to Jesus Christ is beyond human understanding, and those who make peace with themselves and others are following God's mandates.

-Patience-

Patience means not trying to force things to happen, but allowing them to happen in their proper time. The word patience means slow to anger. If we want God's best, we will wait for God's best.

We all know people who are short-tempered and lose their patience quickly. The Bible tells us that patience is long-suffering, forbearance, and perseverance. With patience it is necessary to instill a sense of peace and calmness at the same time.

> Exodus 34:5–7—Then the LORD came down in a cloud and stood there with him; and he called out his own name, Yahweh. The LORD passed in front of Moses, calling out, "Yahweh! The Lord! The God of compassion and mercy! I am slow to anger and filled with unfailing love and faithfulness. I lavish unfailing love to a thousand generations. I forgive iniquity, rebellion, and sin. But I do not excuse the guilty.

> Romans 2:3–4—Since you judge others for doing these things, why do you think you

can avoid God's judgment when you do the same things? Don't you see how wonderfully kind, tolerant, and patient God is with you? Does this mean nothing to you? Can't you see that his kindness is intended to turn you from your sin?

Many people today are not patient in this I want it now world, yet we know the best things come to those who wait for the right time. We as Christians must show patience and encourage others to do the same. It is not difficult to trace the source of spiritual patience.

> 1 Corinthians 13:4—Love is patient and kind. Love is not jealous or boastful or proud.

> Luke 8:15—And the seeds that fell on the good soil represent honest, good-hearted people who hear God's Word, cling to it, and patiently produce a huge harvest.

-Kindness-

Kindness is most associated with human interaction. It comes from the Greek word *chrestotes* which implies an active love and compassion towards others.

> Ephesians 4:32—Instead, be kind to each other, tenderhearted, forgiving one another, just as God through Christ has forgiven you.

> Proverbs 3:3—Never let loyalty and kindness leave you! Tie them around your neck as a reminder. Write them deep within your heart.

Kindness should be a part of all of us, even when it takes the sacrifice of personal time and energy. It may require discipline to be thoughtful of the needs of others and to make the effort to act on those needs, but it is essential to know that God requires it. How much is required to smile, to open a door, to let someone with fewer items in front of you in line, to say a word of encouragement, to comfort someone with your words, or to show friendliness by warmly and sincerely greeting someone?

Acts of kindness are immeasurable—like love, kindness can reach out and touch the lives of those far removed from the original act. Kindness is sowing seeds others are able to harvest.

It is easy to be kind to those you like and those who like you. Are you willing to put aside your pride to be kind to someone you know will not be kind in return?

-Goodness-

What do you think of when you hear the word goodness or the phrase a good person or a good job? It refers to something that meets a high standard of excellence.

God's goodness is a part of His Holy nature. Man's goodness is a quality that comes from serving God. When believers are filled with the Holy Spirit, they are to nurture this goodness given to them by God into a positive expression of their own Christ-like personality. This goodness is similar to kindness, but with an emphasis on high moral standards.

> Luke 6:45—A good person produces good things from the treasury of a good heart, and an evil person produces evil things from the treasury of an evil heart. What you say flows from what is in your heart.

Goodness was personified in the life of Jesus Christ, and Christians are to exemplify this holy goodness by teaching and preaching the Word of God, encouraging and serving others, and having fellowship with believers.

> Galatians 6:9–10—So let's not get tired of doing what is good. At just the right time we will reap a harvest of blessing if we don't give up. Therefore, whenever we have the opportunity, we should do good to everyone—especially to those in the family of faith.

> Romans 12:9–13—Don't just pretend to love others. Really love them. Hate what is wrong. Hold tightly to what is good. Love each other with genuine affection, and take delight in honoring each other. Never be lazy, but work hard and serve the Lord enthusiastically. Rejoice in our confident hope. Be patient in

trouble, and keep on praying. When God's people are in need, be ready to help them. Always be eager to practice hospitality.

-Faithfulness-

Faithfulness teaches us about the loyal and trusting side of life. A large number of synonyms can be related to 'faithfulness,' which gives an understanding of the word in more specific terms.

Webster's New World Dictionary defines faithful as "maintaining allegiance; constant; loyal; marked by or showing a strong sense of duty or responsibility; conscientious; accurate; reliable; exact."

Faithfulness can be seen as both an attitude and an action shown toward God and others. As with any spiritual fruit, Jesus is the standard of faithfulness we are to measure ourselves by. Jesus' faithfulness is shown and demonstrated throughout the Bible. Jesus was faithful even unto death.

> Deuteronomy 7:9—Understand, therefore, that the LORD your God is indeed God. He is the faithful God who keeps his covenant for a thousand generations and lavishes his unfailing love on those who love him and obey his commands.
>
> Psalms 31:23—Love the LORD, all you godly ones! For the LORD protects those who are

loyal to him, but he harshly punishes the arrogant.

2 Thessalonians 3:3—But the Lord is faithful; he will strengthen you and guard you from the evil one.?

God's very nature and character constitute a sacred obligation that He will stand by His Word, that He is bound by His character and that He can never be, even in the smallest degree contrary to His Holy Nature. We as humans do not always choose to do the same thing the same way, but God never wavers in what He chooses to do. God's character never changes. He is always faithful in carrying out what He says He will do.

Hebrews 10:23—Let us hold tightly without wavering to the hope we affirm, for God can be trusted to keep his promise.

-Gentleness-

Gentleness is a goodness of character given to us by God. Paul tells us "as God's chosen people we are to clothe ourselves with gentleness and the other spiritual virtues."

Colossians 3:12—Since God chose you to be the holy people he loves, you must clothe yourselves with tenderhearted mercy, kindness, humility, gentleness, and patience.

1 Peter 3:15–16—Instead, you must worship Christ as Lord of your life. And if someone asks about your hope as a believer, always be ready to explain it. But do this in a gentle and respectful way. Keep your conscience clear. Then, if people speak against you, they will be ashamed when they see what a good life you live because you belong to Christ.

Gentleness of spirit enables us to be patient with those who insult or degrade us. It allows us to endure provocation without being insulted or injured by it. It allows us to remain calm when someone is showing anger towards us. Gentle people do not seek revenge.

-Self-control-

Self-control (temperance) is listed last, but there is no doubt about its importance for Christian living. Can Christians be uncontrolled in their manner of life and still show their love for God? Not really!

The Greek word for self-control, *egkrate* means to possess power, to be strong, and to be the master of your feelings and emotions. Self-control is letting your spiritual nature take control, giving you the ability to use discipline and restraint when dealing with others. In the book of Proverbs it tells us that conquering yourself is greater than a man who conquers a city.

> Proverbs 16:32—Better to be patient than powerful; better to have self-control than to conquer a city.

Paul, in his letter to the Corinthians tells us he disciplines his body to do what he wants it to do.

> 1 Corinthians 9:27—I discipline my body like an athlete, training it to do what it should. Otherwise, I fear that after preaching to others I myself might be disqualified.

On the surface, being a Christian appears easy, but that is not always the case. When a Christian follows the example Jesus set for us, there will be times of adversity, trial, and sacrifice.

> 2 Peter 1:6—And knowledge with self-control, and self-control with patient endurance, and patient endurance with godliness.

> 2 Timothy 3:12—Yes, and everyone who wants to live a godly life in Christ Jesus will suffer persecution.

Sowing Spiritual Fruit

When we apply the Fruit of the Spirit in our lives, we are able to manifest God's love in us and through us. God tells us to:

- Care for each other with love and respect.

  Matthew 7:12—"Do to others whatever you would like them to do to you. This is the essence of all that is taught in the law and the prophets.

  Luke 6:31—Do to others as you would like them to do to you.

- Practice deeds of love and kindness to all of God's creation.

  Colossians 3:12—Since God chose you to be the holy people he loves, you must clothe yourselves with tenderhearted mercy, kindness, humility, gentleness, and patience.

- Do not judge (condemn) one another or you will be judged.

  Romans 14:12–13—Yes, each of us will give a personal account to God. So let's stop condemning (judging) each other. Decide instead to live in such a way that you will not cause another believer to stumble and fall.

Matthew 7:1–2—Do not judge others, and you will not be judged. For you will be treated as you treat others. The standard you use in judging is the standard by which you will be judged.

We must take care not to judge or condemn others, when doing so may cause them harm or loss of faith.

- Do not be consumed with anger and hate for one another.

    Galatians 5:15—But if you are always biting and devouring one another, watch out! Beware of destroying one another.

Being involved in bitter arguments, dissension, gossip, and other nonconstructive behaviors lead you down a destructive path that holds at least part of your spirit in bondage.

- Do not boast.

    Psalms 12:3—May the Lord cut off their flattering lips and silence their boastful tongues.

2 Timothy 3:2—For people will love only themselves and their money. They will be boastful and proud, scoffing at God, disobedient to their parents, and ungrateful. They will consider nothing sacred.

2 Peter 2:18—They brag about themselves with empty, foolish boasting. With an appeal to twisted sexual desires, they lure back into sin those who have barely escaped from a lifestyle of deception.

- Do not speak evil against one another.

James 4:11—Don't speak evil against each other, dear brothers and sisters. If you criticize and judge each other, then you are criticizing and judging God's law. But your job is to obey the law, not to judge whether it applies to you.

We are not to let distractions derail or remove us from the awesome plan God has for our lives or to distract us from the job He has called us to do.

Ephesians 5:8–10

For once you were full of darkness, but now you have light from the Lord. So live as people of light! For this light within you produces only what is good and right and true. Carefully determine what pleases the Lord.

Chapter Seven

A Leap of Faith

Hebrews 11:1
Faith shows the reality of what we hope for; it is the evidence of things we cannot see.

Romans 10:17
So faith comes from hearing, that is, hearing the Good News about Christ.

Biblical Faith

The Merriam-Webster Dictionary defines faith as a strong belief or trust in someone or something. Although this is true, it is not the biblical faith required to serve a loving God. The Greek word used for faith is *pistis*. When the word *pistis* is translated into English in the Bible, different words are used in its place depending on the context in which it is used—belief, faith, faithfulness, fidelity, conviction, confidence, pledge, proof, assurance or trust.

> Colossians 1:23—But you must continue (in faith) to believe (pistis) this truth and stand firmly in it. Don't drift away from the assurance you received when you heard the Good News. The Good News has been preached all over the world, and I, Paul, have been appointed as God's servant to proclaim it.

One must believe that someone or something exists before it is possible to have faith in that person or thing. However, I can have faith in things that do not exist, like when I was young I believed in the Easter Bunny and my faith was confirmed every Easter morning with a basket full of candy. I can also have faith in things that do not affect my life. I have faith that the moon will always be there at night, even if I am not able to see it, but I do not live my life differently because of that faith. This type of faith falls way short of biblical faith.

There are people who believe in hell, but that does not change who they are or how they live. Satan believes in God, yet he continues to rob, kill and destroy. Faith without the salvation of Jesus Christ is an empty faith.

There are different levels of biblical faith:

- No Faith.

   Mark 4:40—Then he asked them, "Why are you afraid? Do you still have no faith?"

- Little Faith.

   Matthew 6:30—And if God cares so wonderfully for wildflowers that are here today and thrown into the fire tomorrow, he will certainly care for you. Why do you have so little faith?

- Great Faith.

   Matthew 8:10—When Jesus heard this, he was amazed. Turning to those who were following him, he said, "I tell you the truth, I haven't seen (such great) faith like this in all Israel!

- Full of Faith.

   Acts 6:5—Everyone liked this idea, and they chose the following: Stephen (a man full of faith and the Holy Spirit), Philip, Procorus, Nicanor, Timon, Parmenas, and Nicolas of Antioch (an early convert to the Jewish faith).

- Healing Faith.

Acts 14:9—And listening as Paul preached. Looking straight at him, Paul realized he had faith to be healed.

James 5:14-15—Are any of you sick? You should call for the elders of the church to come and pray over you, anointing you with oil in the name of the Lord. Such a prayer offered in faith will heal the sick, and the Lord will make you well. And if you have committed any sins, you will be forgiven.

- Sanctifying Faith.

Acts 26:18—To open their eyes, so they may turn from darkness to light and from the power of Satan to God. Then they will receive forgiveness for their sins and be given a place among God's people, who are set apart by (their sanctifying faith in Jesus) faith in me.'

- Righteous Faith.

Romans 3:22—We are made right with God by placing our (righteous) faith in Jesus Christ. And this is true for everyone who believes, no matter who we are.

Today, many people believe that a simple faith in God is enough to insure their blissful place in heaven. Yet, they have not accepted the salvation offered by God's Son, Jesus Christ, nor do they live according to His Word. Biblical faith begins by accepting the salvation offered by Jesus Christ, adherence to His teachings and following in His footsteps.

There are seven essential parts that make up the foundation of biblical faith—a saving faith.

1. Know that your Christian roots are anchored firmly in a solid relationship with the God of Abraham, Isaac and Jacob.

    Matthew 22:32—'I am the God of Abraham, the God of Isaac, and the God of Jacob.' So he is the God of the living, not the dead."

2. Know what God expects from you and what you can expect from Him as you live your life under His authority.

    Matthew 28:18–20—Jesus came and told his disciples, "I have been given all authority in heaven and on earth. Therefore, go and make disciples of all the nations, baptizing them in the name of the Father and the Son and the Holy Spirit. Teach these new disciples to obey all the commands I have given you. And be sure of this: I am with you always, even to the end of the age."

3. Know and follow the instructions and teachings of your Heavenly Father.

Luke 11:28—Jesus replied, "But even more blessed are all who hear the Word of God and put it into practice."

4. Know how God communicates with His people.

- Through Theophanies (Exodus 3:21)
- Through Angels (Luke 1:26–28)
- Through an Audible Voice (Acts 9:4–5)
- Through Visions (Acts 10:9–18)
- Through Dreams (Matthew 1:20–21)
- Through the Holy Spirit (Acts 16:6–7)
- Through Prophets (Hebrews 1:1)
- Through His Holy Word (2 Timothy 3:16)
- Through His Son, Jesus Christ (Hebrews 1:2)

5. Know what God has done in the past for His people He can do for you.

Ecclesiastes 3:15—What is happening now has happened before, and what will happen in the future has happened before, because God makes the same things happen over and over again.

6. Know that God does not change and will never go against what He has ever done or said.

> Numbers 23:19—God is not human, that he should lie, not a human being, that he should change his mind. Does he speak and then not act? Does he promise and not fulfill?

> Hebrews 13:8—Jesus Christ is the same yesterday, today, and forever.

7. Know that your future is secure in Him.

> Jeremiah 29:11—For I know the plans I have for you, says the LORD. They are plans for good and not for disaster, to give you a future and a hope.

Faith versus Works

Many Christians use the following scripture to justify that good works are not necessary to support a Christian faith.

> Ephesians 2:8–10—God saved you by his grace when you believed. And you can't take credit for this; it is a gift from God. Salvation is not a reward for the good things we have done, so none of us can boast about it. For we are God's masterpiece. He has created us

> anew in Christ Jesus, so we can do the good things he planned for us long ago.
>
> James 2:20—How foolish! Can't you see that faith without good deeds (works) is useless?
>
> James 2:18—Now someone may argue, "Some people have faith; others have good deeds." But I say, "How can you show me your faith if you don't have good deeds? I will show you my faith by my good deeds."

The above scripture tells us there is no way to earn salvation through works alone; it is a gift of God's grace. And this is true! But Jesus makes it clear that we are saved for good works, not by good works. After being saved, we become a part of Christ's royal priesthood and our testimony of salvation is by our deeds based on faith.

> 1 Peter 2:9—But you are not like that, for you are a chosen people. You are royal priests, a holy nation, God's very own possession. As a result, you can show others the goodness of God, for he called you out of the darkness into his wonderful light.
>
> Matthew 7:21—"Not everyone who calls out to me, 'Lord! Lord!' will enter the Kingdom of Heaven. Only those who actually do the will of my Father in heaven will enter.

Although our faith can only be accessed through God's grace, it is only by God's grace we are able to live the life He has prepared for us.

> Romans 5:1–2—Therefore, since we have been made right in God's sight by faith, we have peace with God because of what Jesus Christ our Lord has done for us. Because of our faith, Christ has brought us into this place of undeserved privilege where we now stand, and we confidently and joyfully look forward to sharing God's glory.

God is Faithful

We can believe in God, but not have the faith that He is faithful to do what He says He will do, every time, without fail. God would like all His children to believe in Him and have the faith that His Word is true, but sadly this is not always the case.

> 1 Corinthians 1:9—God will do this, for he is faithful to do what he says, and he has invited you into partnership with his Son, Jesus Christ our Lord.

> Romans 3:3–4—True, some of them were unfaithful; but just because they were unfaithful, does that mean God will be unfaithful? Of course not! Even if everyone

else is a liar, God is true. As the Scriptures say about him, "You will be proved right in what you say, and you will win your case in court."

An idle faith is the conviction that something is true without necessarily having any proof, substance or evidence behind it. Fairy tales often claim that all you have to do is believe, and you can make anything come true. Unfortunately, this is how some believers view their faith. All you need to do is to believe, and belief alone will make it happen.

However, when a belief is backed up by proof, substance, or evidence it reaches the level of faith. Faith attains the level of biblical faith when you live out the life of Christ by following in His footsteps.

> John 7:38—Anyone who believes in me may come and drink! For the Scriptures declare, 'Rivers of living water will flow from his heart.'

> Luke 6:46—"So why do you keep calling me 'Lord, Lord!' when you don't do what I say?

> Proverbs 14:15—Only simpletons believe everything they're told! The prudent carefully consider their steps.

Biblical faith means one is putting his or her absolute belief in Jesus based on the knowledge that He is able to do what He said He will do. Who or what one places their faith in can have far-reaching, even eternal consequences.

Faith opens the door to another way of thinking and living when it is used to serve our Creator. Faith is also a living experience centered on spiritual meaning, divine ideals, eternal hope, high moral values and performing the supernatural feats Jesus said we would be able to do.

Being Faithful is an Expression of Love

Love is the highest expression of our faith in God. When we have faith in God's love for us, we can clearly see and hear Him. As we share God's Love, those who are among His followers will listen and apply the love that comes from their faith. In 1 John 4, the Apostle John binds love and faith together in a very insightful and meaningful way.

1 John 4

> Dear friends, do not believe everyone who claims to speak by the Spirit. You must test them to see if the spirit they have comes from God. For there are many false prophets in the world. This is how we know if they have the Spirit of God: If a person claiming to be a prophet acknowledges that Jesus Christ came in a real body, that person has the Spirit of God. But if someone claims to be a prophet and does not acknowledge the truth about

Jesus, that person is not from God. Such a person has the spirit of the Antichrist, which you heard is coming into the world and indeed is already here. But you belong to God, my dear children. You have already won a victory over those people, because the Spirit who lives in you is greater than the spirit who lives in the world. Those people belong to this world, so they speak from the world's viewpoint, and the world listens to them. But we belong to God, and those who know God listen to us. If they do not belong to God, they do not listen to us. That is how we know if someone has the Spirit of truth or the spirit of deception.

Dear friends, let us continue to love one another, for love comes from God. Anyone who loves is a child of God and knows God. But anyone who does not love does not know God, for God is love. God showed how much he loved us by sending his one and only Son into the world so that we might have eternal life through him. This is real love—not that we loved God, but that he loved us and sent his Son as a sacrifice to take away our sins.

Dear friends, since God loved us that much, we surely ought to love each other. No one has ever seen God. But if we love each other,

God lives in us, and his love is brought to full expression in us. And God has given us his Spirit as proof that we live in him and he in us. Furthermore, we have seen with our own eyes and now testify that the Father sent his Son to be the Savior of the world. All who declare that Jesus is the Son of God have God living in them, and they live in God. We know how much God loves us, and we have put our trust in his love. God is love, and all who live in love live in God, and God lives in them. And as we live in God, our love grows more perfect. So we will not be afraid on the day of judgment, but we can face him with confidence because we live like Jesus here in this world. Such love has no fear, because perfect love expels all fear. If we are afraid, it is for fear of punishment, and this shows that we have not fully experienced his perfect love. We love each other because he loved us first. If someone says, "I love God," but hates a fellow believer, that person is a liar; for if we don't love people we can see, how can we love God, whom we cannot see? And he has given us this command: Those who love God must also love their fellow believers.

Everyone who expresses God's love is born of God and knows God. The word used to express God's love in a social and moral sense is taken from the Greek word "agape" which means the absolute love of God (divine love). It is the love God put into His creation. Without the love God imparted to His creation, human love is not possible. Agape is the love we as Christians are to demonstrate and show towards others; unselfishly, unreserved, unconditionally and without reservation.

> 1 John 4:8—But anyone who does not love (agape) does not know God, for God is love.

> 1 John 4:19-20—If someone says, "I love God," but hates a fellow believer, that person is a liar; for if we don't love people we can see, how can we love God, whom we cannot see? And he has given us this command: Those who love God must also love their fellow believers.

Stepping Out On Faith

Acts of Faith are to be performed under the authority given to Jesus by His Father. Jesus directly addressed the issue of where His authority came from in the book of John.

> John 7:16—So Jesus told them, "My message is not my own; it comes from God who sent me.

> John 12:49–50—I don't speak on my own authority. The Father who sent me has commanded me what to say and how to say it. And I know his commands lead to eternal life; so I say whatever the Father tells me to say.

> John 14:24—Anyone who doesn't love me will not obey me. And remember, my words are not my own. What I am telling you is from the Father who sent me.

After Jesus' resurrection, God the Father gave to Jesus the right to command both the earthly realm and the spiritual realm. As a result, both realms are obligated to obey Jesus' commands and submit to His authority.

> Matthew 28:18—Jesus came and told his disciples, "I have been given all authority in heaven and on earth.

We see Jesus' faith in the Garden of Gethsemane before His crucifixion.

> Matthew 26:36–39—Then Jesus went with them to the olive grove called Gethsemane, and he said, "Sit here while I go over there to pray." He took Peter and Zebedee's two sons, James and John, and he became anguished and distressed. He told them, "My soul is crushed with grief to the point of death. Stay

here and keep watch with me." He went on a little farther and bowed with his face to the ground, praying, "My Father! If it is possible, let this cup of suffering be taken away from me. Yet I want your will to be done, not mine."

An Act of Faith—Peter Walks on Water

Peter, the adventurous disciple, had complete trust that Jesus would allow him to walk on the water and not sink. What if Peter believed Jesus could do this but was afraid to get out of the boat? I am sure the other disciples in the boat believed Jesus, but Peter was the only one who stepped out on faith. I am sure Peter was afraid, but his faith in Jesus and his desire to walk on water overcame his fear. Peter took a leap of faith because he knew Jesus had the divine power to keep him afloat. Peter knew that to overcome fear you have to face your fears, no matter the outcome. Look what happened when Peter's fear became too great and he began to doubt Jesus, he began to sink. But who caught him and kept him from drowning. Jesus respects the fact that we step out on faith, even if our faith is not sufficient He will be there for us.

> Matthew 14:28–33—Then Peter called to him, "Lord, if it's really you, tell me to come to you, walking on the water." "Yes, come," Jesus said. So Peter went over the side of the boat and walked on the water toward Jesus.

> But when he saw the strong wind and the waves, he was terrified and began to sink. "Save me, Lord!" he shouted. Jesus immediately reached out and grabbed him. "You have so little faith," Jesus said. "Why did you doubt me?" When they climbed back into the boat, the wind stopped. Then the disciples worshiped him. "You really are the Son of God!" they exclaimed.

Doubt, fear, and unbelief render faith ineffective and play a large part today in a Christian's inability to follow Jesus' commands and to do the supernatural things He told us we would be able to do. Jesus gave us the authority to heal the sick, cast out demons, and raise the dead.

> Matthew 10:1—Jesus called his twelve disciples together and gave them authority to cast out evil spirits and to heal every kind of disease and illness.

> Matthew 10:8—Heal the sick, raise the dead, cure those with leprosy, and cast out demons. Give as freely as you have received!

If we truly are Christians, dedicated followers of Jesus Christ, we will know that our existence is to glorify God in this world and in the next. We are to step out on faith and let Jesus do the rest.

Biblical Criteria for Examining the Genuineness of Our Faith

A biblical faith (saving faith) is composed of many scriptural essential elements which define the essence of a spiritual relationship with Jesus Christ.

- Knowing without a doubt God is true to His Word.

  Deuteronomy 7:9—Understand, therefore, that the LORD your God is indeed God. He is the faithful God who keeps his covenant for a thousand generations and lavishes his unfailing love on those who love him and obey his commands.

- A faith without doubt is required to do the works Jesus commanded us to do.

  Matthew 21:21—Then Jesus told them, "I tell you the truth, if you have faith and don't doubt, you can do things like this and much more. You can even say to this mountain, 'May you be lifted up and thrown into the sea,' and it will happen.

- Faith is to be earnestly defended.

    Jude 1:3—Dear friends, I had been eagerly planning to write to you about the salvation we all share. But now I find that I must write about something else, urging you to defend the faith that God has entrusted once for all time to his holy people.

- Faith comes from our assurance of salvation.

    Ephesians 2:8—God saved you (through faith) by his grace when you believed. And you can't take credit for this; it is a gift from God.

- Faith justifies us before God.

    Romans 5:1:4—Therefore, since we have been made right in God's sight by faith, we have peace with God because of what Jesus Christ our Lord has done for us. Because of our faith, Christ has brought us into this place of undeserved privilege where we now stand, and we confidently and joyfully look forward to sharing God's glory. We can rejoice, too, when we run into problems and trials, for we know that they help us develop endurance. And endurance develops strength of character, and character strengthens our confident hope of salvation.

- Faith is counted as righteousness.

Romans 1:16–17—For I am not ashamed of this Good News about Christ. It is the power of God at work, saving everyone who believes—the Jew first and also the Gentile. This Good News tells us how God makes us right in his sight. This is accomplished from start to finish by faith. As the Scriptures say, "It is through faith that a righteous person has life."

- Faith is healing the afflicted.

James 5:13–16—Are any of you suffering hardships? You should pray. Are any of you happy? You should sing praises. Are any of you sick? You should call for the elders of the church to come and pray over you, anointing you with oil in the name of the Lord. Such a prayer offered in faith will heal the sick, and the Lord will make you well. And if you have committed any sins, you will be forgiven. Confess your sins to each other and pray for each other so that you may be healed. The earnest prayer of a righteous person has great power and produces wonderful results.

God's Faithfulness

Is God faithful? Yes. God's love for us is without measure, and an attribute of His abounding love is faithfulness. God cannot be anything but faithful; it is a part of who He is. Does God require faithfulness from His children? Yes!

> Deuteronomy 7:9–11—Understand, therefore, that the LORD your God is indeed God. He is the faithful God who keeps his covenant for a thousand generations and lavishes his unfailing love on those who love him and obey his commands. But he does not hesitate to punish and destroy those who reject him. Therefore, you must obey all these commands, decrees, and regulations I am giving you today.

God tells us that as long as we do our part, by adhering to His will and following His commandments, He will do His part. Our faithfulness is to be embraced, seized and to be seen by others. Faith without good deeds is dead.

> James 2:14–17—What good is it, dear brothers and sisters, if you say you have faith but don't show it by your actions? Can that kind of faith save anyone? Suppose you see a brother or sister who has no food or clothing,

and you say, "Good-bye and have a good day; stay warm and eat well"—but then you don't give that person any food or clothing. What good does that do? So you see, faith by itself isn't enough. Unless it produces good deeds, it is dead and useless.

There are numerous scriptures pointing to God's faithfulness. The following are a few verses that convey God's love through His faithfulness.

- He protects us.

    2 Thessalonians 3:3—But the Lord is faithful; he will strengthen you and guard you from the evil one.

- He chose us.

    Ephesians 1:4—Even before he made the world, God loved us and chose us in Christ to be holy and without fault in his eyes.

- He called us.

    1 Corinthians 1:9—God will do this, for he is faithful to do what he says, and he has invited (called) you into partnership with his Son, Jesus Christ our Lord.

- He always provides a path out of temptation.

It is important to note here, that God gives you the strength you need to overcome temptation. He does not give you a way out of every tribulation you face in life.

1 Corinthians 10:13—The temptations in your life are no different from what others experience. And God is faithful. He will not allow the temptation to be more than you can stand. When you are tempted, he will show you a way out so that you can endure.

- He loves us.

Deuteronomy 7:9—Understand, therefore, that the LORD your God is indeed God. He is the faithful God who keeps his covenant for a thousand generations and lavishes his unfailing love on those who love him and obey his commands.

Testing Your Faith

How can you know if your faith is genuine? Examine your life based on the character of Jesus. Do you see His character in you? Do you have God's love inside you? There are people today who hold to a faith that does not follow in the footsteps of Jesus. This is sometimes referred to as "blind faith" "dead faith" or "empty faith."

> James 2:26—Just as the body is dead without breath, so also faith is dead without good works.

God allows our faith to be tested because He wants our faith to be steadfast and without doubt.

> James 1:2-3—Dear brothers and sisters, when troubles of any kind come your way, consider it an opportunity for great joy. For you know that when your faith is tested, your endurance has a chance to grow.

> 2 Corinthians 13:5—Examine yourselves to see if your faith is genuine. Test yourselves. Surely you know that Jesus Christ is among you; if not, you have failed the test of genuine faith.

The New Testament provides very practical ways to determine whether we are of the fold of Christ or not. Take the test yourself. Check to see whether you pass the test.

- Are you able to hear the Word of God?
- Are you faithful to the Word of God?
- Do you love everyone? No exceptions!

A Leap of Faith

- More specifically, do you love yourself and have you truly forgiven yourself for past transgressions?
- Can you truthfully confess that Jesus is the Son of God; that He was born of a virgin, died and was resurrected?
- Do you trust that God will keep His promises?
- Do you see God working in your life?
- Have you ever stepped out on faith, believing God will do what He said He would do?

All Christians should make a lifetime commitment to base their lives on the Word of God and the life of Jesus, God will honor this commitment.

We are all given different gifts and abilities to promote the glory of God. We honor our gifts and abilities from God by putting our faith into action. Take a leap of faith, step out and work with Jesus in the supernatural.

Galatians 2:20

My old self has been crucified with Christ. It is no longer I who live, but Christ (who) lives in me. So I live in this earthly body by trusting (having faith) in the Son of God, who loved me and gave himself (His life) for me.

Chapter Eight

Heaven is a Real Place

2 Corinthians 5:1–5
For we know that when this earthly tent we live in is taken down (that is, when we die and leave this earthly body), we will have a house in heaven, an eternal body made for us by God himself and not by human hands. We grow weary in our present bodies, and we long to put on our heavenly bodies like new clothing. For we will put on heavenly bodies; we will not be spirits without bodies. While we live in these earthly bodies, we groan and sigh, but it's not that we want to die and get rid of these bodies that clothe us. Rather, we want to put on our new bodies so that these dying bodies will be swallowed up by life. God himself has prepared us for this, and as a guarantee he has given us his Holy Spirit.

What does the Bible tell us about Heaven?

Most Christians embrace the understanding derived from God's Word that even nonscientific methods and reasoning do bring an understanding and knowledge of the purposes our Creator built into His creation. However, it is only through divine revelation and our response to it that we can begin our journey to see into the spiritual world. We are going to explore the adventures of those who have seen and experienced many exciting and not so exciting worlds beyond our own. These revelations have left no doubt that we are truly spiritual and immortal beings. Knowledge of these worlds is available to anyone who seeks to know of their existence.

The many places in heaven are not merely imagined or invented to give people hope amidst the pain and suffering of this world. Heaven is for real! As Jesus demonstrated by his resurrection, death is not an end, but merely an entrance into another life. During the last supper with His disciples, Jesus told them He was going to prepare a place for them in God's Kingdon.

Christians believe the biblical heaven "Paradise" is a definite place where they will spend eternity with Jesus.

- Heaven was Jesus' home before His Incarnation.

    John 6:38—For I (Jesus) have come down from heaven to do the will of God who sent me, not to do my own will.

- Heaven is the place Jesus returned to after His resurrection.

    Luke 24:51—While he was blessing them, he left them and was taken up to heaven.

In the narrative of The Last Supper, a verse that is often overlooked is where Jesus tells His disciples they will be with Him in heaven.

    Matthew 26:29—Mark my words—I will not drink wine again until the day I drink it new with you in my Father's Kingdom."

This scripture tells us that:

- Heaven is a real place.
- We will be with Jesus in heaven.
- We will have a recognizable spiritual body.
- We will be able to eat and drink there.

The Apostle John, in the book of Revelations tells us that we will rest from our earthly labors, and our earthly good works will go with us into heaven.

    Revelations 14:13—And I heard a voice from heaven saying, "Write this down: Blessed are those who die in the Lord from now on. Yes, says the Spirit, they are blessed indeed, for they will rest from their hard work; for their good deeds (works) follow them!"

Although Scripture discusses heaven in many terms, it is not possible to understand the full nature of heaven by reading the Bible. I have studied many ancient Christian and Jewish manuscripts and the "Heavenly" experiences of many reliable people to shed light on what heaven may be like. I have tried to be careful and not present anything that would go against God's Holy Word. If there is any question as to what the heavenly realms may be like, the Bible is the final Word. I hope you enjoy the tour.

The Early Church

The Nag Hammadi texts discovered in 1945 and the discovery of the Dead Sea Scrolls in 1947, have given scholars a more in-depth picture of early Jewish and Christian cultures that give a richer understanding of Scripture.

There are many books out today that discuss the early Christian Church and its many beliefs. These books tell us how early Christians understood their faith and how the teachings of Jesus were interpreted and followed. Most of these beliefs are the same as those taught by what is considered Orthodox Christianity today.

However, some early texts that were considered sacred by the followers of Jesus were seen as being too mystical and were left out of today's Bible. The early

Church believed in prophecies, visions and visitations from the spiritual world. They demonstrated the supernatural and miraculous power of God as they spread the Gospel of Jesus. It was all about Jesus and what He taught. They lived and experienced the supernatural while teaching others to do the same.

Some of the highly held beliefs that were revered among many early Christians are:

- Christianity is foremost a spiritual journey to seek the deeper truths of God.
- A Christian is to always seek the moral high ground.
- A Christian is to be a seeker of truth rather than claiming to have the exclusive truth.
- Knowing yourself is crucial to knowing God.
- The act of loving others comes before spreading the Gospel
- Christian truth is open to debate and should be sought after.
- Claiming exclusive truth is not faith, not love, and not honest.
- It is far more important to seek God through knowledge rather than to "just believe in His existence."
- Belief was a basic foundation to build upon. No one had the final truth when it came to living a godly life. Jesus' message was spiritual not religious and only "God the Father," Not Man, has all the answers.

- The first place to find God was within oneself, not in the doctrines or the dictates of Man.
- Faith is not so much what you believe about Jesus, but how you respond to His life and His teachings. By continually seeking to bring Jesus into your life, you will be transformed by the power of His Spirit. Continually seeking to be like Jesus was the true act of faith and the hope of eternal life. Belief became faith when you put the words of Jesus into action.

If you look at the true mystics, miracle workers, and prophets of the Early Church, you will find people whose life experiences were centered on the teachings of Jesus. They were totally devoted to Jesus and would readily give their lives for their belief; there was no plan "B." When you read the accounts of these people who saw Jesus, spread the Gospel, worked miracles, and performed signs and wonders, it is hard to imagine that some churches today are part of the same family. Where are those today who walk in the footsteps of Jesus—as recorded in His Holy Word?

> Matthew 10:38If you refuse to take up your cross and follow me, you are not worthy of being mine.

> Deuteronomy 13:4—Serve only the LORD your God and fear him alone. Obey his commands, listen to his voice, and cling to him.

A spiritual journey into the world where God lives

>Ephesians 2:10—For we are God's masterpiece. He has created us anew in Christ Jesus, so we can do the good things he planned for us long ago.
>
>John 13:35—Your love for one another will prove to the world that you are my disciples.
>
>Colossians 3:17—And whatever you do or say, do it as a representative of the Lord Jesus, giving thanks through him to God the Father.

In today's Church we think we understand Jesus when we study the biblical concepts that define Him. In the early church, to experience Jesus was to model your life after Him. Understanding Jesus came through revelatory moments and experiences, not intellectual concepts. Paul told us to fix our eyes on not what is seen, but on what is unseen. How do we see what is unseen? We start by putting our faith, trust, and the life of Jesus into action. Jesus now lives in the spiritual world and we are to worship Him in spirit. Jesus is the key that opens the door to a Spirit filled life.

The Pharisees (Priests) in Jesus' time knew God by the written Word, yet their lifestyle lacked a true relationship with Him. They had full knowledge of the biblical laws, but were unable to see or hear in the spirit. Jesus called them hypocrites. How many Christians do you know today that hear the "Word," but do not act on it?

- Matthew 23:13—What sorrow awaits you teachers of religious law and you Pharisees. Hypocrites! For you shut the door of the Kingdom of Heaven in people's faces. You won't go in yourselves, and you don't let others enter either.

My kingdom is not of This World

- The Christian's "hope" is to be realized "in the heavens."

  - Colossians 1:4–5—For we have heard of your faith in Christ Jesus and your love for all of God's people, which come from your confident hope of what God has reserved for you in heaven. You have had this expectation ever since you first heard the truth of the Good News.

- Our place in heaven is eternal and "will not fade away."

  - 1 Peter 1:3–4—All praise to God, the Father of our Lord Jesus Christ. It is by his great mercy that we have been born again, because God raised Jesus Christ from the dead. Now we live with great expectation, and we have a priceless inheritance—an inheritance that is kept in heaven for you, pure and undefiled, beyond the reach of change and decay.

- Jesus makes it clear that heaven is not part of our physical world.

  John 18:36—Jesus answered, "My Kingdom is not an earthly kingdom. If it were, my followers would fight to keep me from being handed over to the Jewish leaders. But my Kingdom is not of this world."

- Jesus transformed into His glorious body before Peter, James, and John.

  Matthew 17:1–3—Six days later Jesus took Peter and the two brothers, James and John, and led them up a high mountain to be alone. As the men watched, Jesus' appearance was transformed so that his face shone like the sun, and his clothes became as white as light. Suddenly, Moses and Elijah appeared and began talking with Jesus.

Although Moses and Elijah had passed away hundreds of years before the transfiguration, they were alive in their spiritual bodies, their resurrected, glorified state. What is not always understood is that Jesus knew them before the transfiguration.

Heaven is a Real Place

The Nature of Our Bodies in Heaven

Paul in his discussions with the church in Corinth tells us what our heavenly bodies will be like. This is probably the most prominent scripture in the Bible concerning how our bodies will be changed to accommodate life in heaven. Our body in heaven will be spiritual, not physical, but it will be recognized as it was in the physical world.

> 1 Corinthians 15:41–50—The sun has one kind of glory, while the moon and stars each have another kind. And even the stars differ from each other in their glory. It is the same way with the resurrection of the dead. Our earthly bodies are planted in the ground when we die, but they will be raised to live forever. Our bodies are buried in brokenness, but they will be raised in glory. They are buried in weakness, but they will be raised in strength. They are buried as natural human bodies, but they will be raised as spiritual bodies. For just as there are natural bodies, there are also spiritual bodies. The Scriptures tell us, "The first man, Adam, became a living person." But the last Adam—that is, Christ—is a life-giving Spirit. What comes first is the natural body, then the spiritual body comes later. Adam, the first man, was made from the dust of the earth, while Christ, the second

man, came from heaven. Earthly people are like the earthly man, and heavenly people are like the heavenly man. Just as we are now like the earthly man, we will someday be like the heavenly man. What I am saying, dear brothers and sisters, is that our physical bodies cannot inherit the Kingdom of God. These dying bodies cannot inherit what will last forever.

Paul, while writing to the Philippians from his prison cell told them that our spiritual bodies will be fashioned like the glorious body of Jesus.

> Philippians 3:21—He will take our weak mortal bodies and change them into glorious bodies like his own, using the same power with which he will bring everything under his control.

- We will be able to Eat and Drink while in Our Spiritual Bodies -

As human beings, we are tethered to a physical and biological world. If we were to lose our physical environment, our physical bodies would die, but our spiritual bodies would live on. Yet our spiritual bodies will still appear similar to the way they did while on earth. While in a glorified form our bodies will have no need for food or drink, but that does not mean we cannot eat or have something to drink if we desire.

There are instances in the Bible where angels, while in human form, and Jesus while in His glorified body ate and drank during their time on earth.

- Mark 14:25—I tell you the truth, I will not drink wine again until the day I drink it new in the Kingdom of God.

- Luke 22:29-30—And just as my Father has granted me a Kingdom, I now grant you the right to eat and drink at my table in my Kingdom. And you will sit on thrones, judging the twelve tribes of Israel.

Salvation Before the Time of Jesus

What about the people of ancient times before the Mosaic Law? What about the people who lived during the time of the Mosaic Law, but never heard of the Law? What about the people who knew the law, but did not abide by it?

Paul tells us that those who have never heard of the law are not subject to the law. Paul also tells us that those who follow the law will be judged by the law. The people who have never heard of the law are judged by how they followed the moral laws God put in their heart and mind.

Romans 2:14-16—Even Gentiles, who do not have God's written law, show that they know his law when they instinctively obey it, even without having heard it. They demonstrate that God's law is written in their hearts, for their own conscience and thoughts either accuse them or tell them they are doing right. And this is the message I proclaim—that the day is coming when God, through Christ Jesus, will judge everyone's secret life.

Romans 4:15—For the law always brings punishment on those who try to obey it.

The Old Testament demonstrates to us that God is both fair and just. Those of the Old Testament, who lived and died before Jesus' earthly ministry went to a place below the earth called Sheol, which was reserved for both the righteous and the unrighteous. Sheol is translated as Hades or Hell in the New Testament.

Jesus' Descent into the Underworld and His Assent into Paradise

While Jesus was on the cross, a thief hanging next to Him, asked to be remembered when Jesus came into His Kingdom.

Luke 23:42-43—Then he said, "Jesus, remember me when you come into your

Kingdom." And Jesus replied, "I assure you, today you will be with me in paradise."

Some theologians believe that when Jesus told the thief He would be with Him in Paradise, He was not referring to Heaven, but to a place in the underworld called Sheol (the state or place of the dead). Other theologians believe Jesus was referring to a place already in the heavens (the Kingdom of God).

Before Jesus' death and resurrection, when people died their bodies were buried and their spirits descended into Sheol—compartments of the dead. In Sheol—also called Hades—there were places for the righteous and places of torment for the unrighteous. Sheol is not a part of the physical world, but has an existence of its own in a lower realm. The Jewish people considered Sheol to be far below the earth's surface.

When Jesus cried out with a loud voice "It is finished," He gave up His earthly body and His Spirit descended into Sheol.

> Matthew 12:40—For as Jonah was in the belly of the great fish for three days and three nights, so will the Son of Man be in the heart of the earth for three days and three nights.

> Proverbs 7:27—Her house is the road to the grave (Sheol). Her bedroom is the den (chambers) of death.

- Sheol—the Conscious realm of those who have died before the death and resurrection of Jesus.

    Ezekiel 32:21—Down in the grave (sheol) mighty leaders will mockingly welcome Egypt and its allies, saying, 'They have come down; they lie among the outcasts, hordes slaughtered by the sword.'

    Isaiah 14:19—but you will be thrown out of your grave like a worthless branch. Like a corpse trampled underfoot, you will be dumped into a mass grave with those killed in battle. You will descend to the pit (Sheol).

    Luke 16:22-23—Finally, the poor man died and was carried by the angels to sit beside Abraham at the heavenly banquet (compartment of the righteous in Sheol). The rich man also died and was buried, and he went to the place of the dead (compartment of the unrighteous in Sheol). There, in torment, he saw Abraham in the far distance with Lazarus at his side.

- The conscious realm of the unrighteous (prison)—a place of torment.

    1 Peter 3:18–19—Christ suffered for our sins once for all time. He never sinned, but

Heaven is a Real Place

- he died for sinners to bring you safely home to God. He suffered physical death, but he was raised to life in the Spirit. So he went and preached to the spirits in prison (the place of the dead in Sheol).

- 1 Peter 4:5–6—But remember that they will have to face God, who stands ready to judge everyone, both the living and the dead. That is why the Good News was preached to those who are now dead—so although they were destined to die like all people, they now live forever with God in the Spirit.

When Jesus left Sheol, he took with him all the believers who had died before his crucifixion and those who repented after receiving His message of salvation. Jesus took them with him to Paridise. The places in Sheol that remain are today referred to as hell.

- Ephesians 4:8–11—That is why the Scriptures say, "When he ascended to the heights, he led a crowd of captives and gave gifts to his people." Notice that it says "he ascended." This clearly means that Christ also descended to our lowly world. And the same one who descended is the one who ascended higher than all the heavens, so that he might fill the entire universe with himself. Now these are the gifts Christ gave to the church: the apostles, the prophets, the evangelists, and the pastors and teachers.

Psalms 68:18—When you ascended to the heights, you led a crowd of captives. You received gifts from the people, even from those who rebelled against you. Now the Lord God will live among us there.

Hosea 13:14—"Should I ransom them from the grave (Sheol)? Should I redeem them from death? O death, bring on your terrors! O grave, bring on your plagues! For I will not take pity on them.

Psalms 16:10—For you will not leave my soul among the dead (Sheol) or allow your holy one to rot in the grave.

Job 14:13—I wish you would hide me in the grave (Sheol) and forget me there until your anger has passed. But mark your calendar to think of me again!

While Jesus was in heaven, He entered the Heavenly Temple to perform one of the most important duties as our High Priest. He entered the Holy of Holies and gave his blood to obtain eternal redemption for those who believe in Him.

Heaven is a Real Place

Hebrews 9:11-14—So Christ has now become the High Priest over all the good things that have come. He has entered that greater, more perfect Tabernacle in heaven, which was not made by human hands and is not part of this created world. With his own blood—not the blood of goats and calves—he entered the Most Holy Place once for all time and secured our redemption forever. Under the old system, the blood of goats and bulls and the ashes of a heifer could cleanse people's bodies from ceremonial impurity. Just think how much more the blood of Christ will purify our consciences from sinful deeds so that we can worship the living God. For by the power of the eternal Spirit, Christ offered himself to God as a perfect sacrifice for our sins.

Hebrews 4:14-16—So then, since we have a great High Priest who has entered heaven, Jesus the Son of God, let us hold firmly to what we believe. This High Priest of ours understands our weaknesses, for he faced all of the same testings we do, yet he did not sin. So let us come boldly to the throne of our gracious God. There we will receive his mercy, and we will find grace to help us when we need it most.

After Jesus had performed his duty as our High Priest, He returned to earth for forty days where He appeared in His spiritual body to His disciples and to over five hundred others.

> 1 Corinthians 15:6—After that, he was seen by more than 500 of his followers at one time, most of whom are still alive, though some have died.

Jesus' Extraordinary Powers while in His Glorified Body

Scripture tells us of several supernatural events that occurred during the forty days Jesus was on earth before His ascension. He was able to appear and disappear at will, travel from one place to another instantaneously, change His appearance, and move through walls—expressing the the abilities of His spiritual body.

- After His resurrection, Jesus first appeared to Mary Magdalene outside the tomb.

    > John 20:17—"Don't cling to me," Jesus said, "for I haven't yet ascended to the Father. But go find my brothers and tell them, 'I am ascending to my Father and your Father, to my God and your God.'"

- Jesus appeared to His disciples when they were together in a room with the doors locked for fear of reprisal from the Jewish leaders.

John 20:19—That Sunday evening the disciples were meeting behind locked doors because they were afraid of the Jewish leaders. Suddenly, Jesus was standing there among them! "Peace be with you," he said.

- Two disciples of Jesus, Cleopas and one unnamed, were walking from Jerusalem to Emmaus on the day that Jesus rose from the dead. As they traveled, Jesus joined them, and they did not recognize Him. As they walked, Jesus taught them about the predictions of His coming and how He fulfilled all of those prophecies. When they arrived in Emmaus that evening, the two disciples stopped to eat, and they asked Jesus to join them. As Jesus broke the bread and gave thanks, "their eyes were opened" and they recognized Him. Jesus then vanished before their eyes.

Luke 24:13–16—That same day two of Jesus' followers were walking to the village of Emmaus, seven miles from Jerusalem. As they walked along they were talking about everything that had happened. As they talked and discussed these things, Jesus himself suddenly came and began walking with them. But God kept them from recognizing him.

Luke 24:28–31—By this time they were nearing Emmaus and the end of their journey. Jesus acted as if he were going on, but they begged him, "Stay the night with us, since it is getting late." So he went home with them. As they sat down to eat, he took the bread and blessed it. Then he broke it and gave it to them. Suddenly, their eyes were opened, and they recognized him. And at that moment he disappeared!

- Jesus, again unrecognized, overwhelmed seven disciples by filling their fishing nets with a huge catch.

John 21:1–7—Later, Jesus appeared again to the disciples beside the Sea of Galilee. This is how it happened. Several of the disciples were there—Simon Peter, Thomas (nicknamed the Twin), Nathanael from Cana in Galilee, the sons of Zebedee, and two other disciples. Simon Peter said, "I'm going fishing." "We'll come, too," they all said. So they went out in the boat, but they caught nothing all night. At dawn Jesus was standing on the beach, but the disciples couldn't see who he was. He called out, "Fellows, have you caught any fish?

"No," they replied. Then he said, "Throw out your net on the right-hand side of the boat, and you'll get some!" So they did, and they couldn't haul in the net because there were so many fish in it. Then the disciple Jesus loved said to Peter, "It's the Lord!" When Simon Peter heard that it was the Lord, he put on his tunic (for he had stripped for work), jumped into the water, and headed to shore.

Jesus' Ascension

Forty days after His resurrection, Jesus in His resurrected body returned to His heavenly home. The books of Mark, Luke and Acts tell the story of His ascension.

> Mark 16:19–20—When the Lord Jesus had finished talking with them, he was taken up into heaven and sat down in the place of honor at God's right hand. And the disciples went everywhere and preached, and the Lord worked through them, confirming what they said by many miraculous signs.

> Luke 24:50–51—Then Jesus led them to Bethany, and lifting his hands to heaven, he blessed them. While he was blessing them, he left them and was taken up to heaven.

> Acts 1:9–11—After saying this, he was taken up into a cloud while they were watching, and they could no longer see him. As they strained to see him rising into heaven, two white-robed men suddenly stood among them. "Men of Galilee," they said, "why are you standing here staring into heaven? Jesus has been taken from you into heaven, but someday he will return from heaven in the same way you saw him go!"

Skeptics allege the resurrection was a conspiracy and Jesus did not really die while on the cross. But many of those who saw Jesus die on the cross and then saw Him again before His ascension, suffered martyrdom for what they knew to be true—Jesus had risen from the dead.

The Judgment Seat of Christ

Everyone from the beginning of time until the end of time, are going to meet Jesus and be judged as to how they led their life—good or bad.

> Hebrews 9:27—And just as each person is destined to die once and after that comes judgment.

> 2 Corinthians 5:10—For we must all stand before Christ to be judged. We will each

receive whatever we deserve for the good or evil we have done in this earthly body.

Romans 14:10—So why do you condemn another believer? Why do you look down on another believer? Remember, we will all stand before the judgment seat of God.

John 5:22–23—In addition, the Father judges no one. Instead, he has given the Son absolute authority to judge, so that everyone will honor the Son, just as they honor the Father. Anyone who does not honor the Son is certainly not honoring the Father who sent him.

Romans 2:5–8—But because you are stubborn and refuse to turn from your sin, you are storing up terrible punishment for yourself. For a day of anger is coming, when God's righteous judgment will be revealed. He will judge everyone according to what they have done. He will give eternal life to those who keep on doing good, seeking after the glory and honor and immortality that God offers. But he will pour out his anger and wrath on those who live for themselves, who refuse to obey the truth and instead live lives of wickedness.

> Matthew 7:21–23—"Not everyone who calls out to me, 'Lord! Lord!' will enter the Kingdom of Heaven. Only those who actually do the will of my Father in heaven will enter. On judgment day many will say to me, 'Lord! Lord! We prophesied in your name, and cast out demons in your name and performed many miracles in your name.' But I will reply, 'I never knew you. Get away from me, you who break God's laws.'

Where is Heaven?

From the beginning of recorded history Man has been searching for heaven: utopia, Shangra-la, Nirvana, the happy hunting grounds, paradise lost, the promised land. Many others believe God and heaven are just states of mind and figments of an overactive imagination.

There are those who believe heaven is here on earth and as humans we are evolving to the perfect nature God intended for us. The decline of the human condition because of overpopulation, pollution, famine, disease and the downward spiral of moral values, tells a different story.

I have come to believe that our place in the afterlife is manifest within us by our moral values and how we live and honor Jesus while here on earth. For those who truly follow in the footsteps of Jesus, upon death their spirit will be transported to their home in the Kingdom of Heaven (the realm called Paradise) where their treasures lie.

> Matthew 6:19–21—Don't store up treasures here on earth, where moths eat them and rust destroys them, and where thieves break in and steal. Store your treasures in heaven, where moths and rust cannot destroy, and thieves do not break in and steal. Wherever your treasure is, there the desires of your heart will also be.

> Luke 12:33–34—"Sell your possessions and give to those in need. This will store up treasure for you in heaven! And the purses of heaven never get old or develop holes. Your treasure will be safe; no thief can steal it and no moth can destroy it. Wherever your treasure is, there the desires of your heart will also be.

Heaven is for Real

Earth is the place where people prepare for the world they will enter after death. The heaven where Jesus lives (Paradise) is the ultimate prize when we accept Him as our personal Lord and Savior. This heavenly kingdom is where Jesus has made His provision available to all who accept His redemptive promise—deliverance from the penalty of sin.

Colossians 1:12–17—Always thanking the Father. He has enabled you to share in the inheritance that belongs to his people, who live in the light. For he has rescued us from the kingdom of darkness and transferred us into the Kingdom of his dear Son, who purchased our freedom and forgave our sins. Christ is the visible image of the invisible God. He existed before anything was created and is supreme over all creation, for through him God created everything in the heavenly realms and on earth. He made the things we can see and the things we can't see—such as thrones, kingdoms, rulers, and authorities in the unseen world. Everything was created through him and for him. He existed before anything else, and he holds all creation together.

Ephesians 1:7—He is so rich in kindness and grace that he purchased our freedom with the blood of his Son and forgave our sins.

Visions of Heaven from the Bible

-Daniel's Vision of Heaven-

Many Bible scholars believe Daniel sees a Theophany, an appearance of Jesus in the Old Testament before He came into the world as the Son of Man—the pre-incarnate Jesus. Scholars base this belief on the description of Jesus in the book of Daniel and confirmed in the book of Revelations.

> Daniel 10:5–8—I looked up and saw a man dressed in linen clothing, with a belt of pure gold around his waist. His body looked like a precious gem. His face flashed like lightning, and his eyes flamed like torches. His arms and feet shone like polished bronze, and his voice roared like a vast multitude of people. Only I, Daniel, saw this vision. The men with me saw nothing, but they were suddenly terrified and ran away to hide.

> Revelation 1:12-16—When I turned to see who was speaking to me, I saw seven gold lampstands. And standing in the middle of the lampstands was someone like the Son of Man. He was wearing a long robe with a gold sash across his chest. His head and his hair were white like wool, as white as snow. And his eyes were like flames of fire. His feet were like polished bronze refined in a furnace, and his voice thundered like mighty ocean waves. He held seven stars in his right hand, and a sharp two-edged sword came from his mouth. And his face was like the sun in all its brilliance.

-Abram's (Abraham) Vision of Heaven-

Genesis 15:1—Some time later, the LORD spoke to Abram in a vision and said to him, "Do not be afraid, Abram, for I will protect you, and your reward will be great."

Stephen, in his trial for blasphemy before the Sanhedrin council confirmed Abraham's vision.

Acts 7:2—This was Stephen's reply: "Brothers and fathers, listen to me. Our glorious God (Shekinah Glory) appeared to our ancestor Abraham in Mesopotamia, before he settled in Haran.

In his vision, Abram saw the Heavenly Glory of God. The Bible does not define specifically what the Glory of God is, but what we do know is when it is seen, it is a manifestation of God that is clearly recognizable. When we see the Glory of God, we know we are in His presence.

-Paul's Vision of Heaven-

Paul, while in the city of Lystra saw a man who had been a cripple from birth. Knowing this man had the faith necessary to be healed, he commanded the man to stand on his feet. The man jumped up and walked. The crowds saw and heard what happened and immediately thought Paul and the other apostles with him were gods.

The apostles immediately told the people they were not gods, only men doing the work of the one true God.

When the apostles would not accept sacrifices made to them, the crowd turned on them. They stoned Paul and dragged his body out of the city where they left him for dead.

> Acts 14:19—Then some Jews arrived from Antioch and Iconium and won the crowds to their side. They stoned Paul and dragged him out of town, thinking he was dead.

It seems that Paul in his letter to the Corinthians was referring to his near-death encounter from the stoning he received in the city of Lystra. He told the Corinthian church of his near-death encounter where he was caught up to heaven.

> 2 Corinthians 12:2–4—I was caught up to the third heaven fourteen years ago. Whether I was in my body or out of my body, I don't know—only God knows. Yes, only God knows whether I was in my body or outside my body. But I do know that I was caught up to paradise and heard things so astounding that they cannot be expressed in words, things no human is allowed to tell.

Paul while on the road to Damascus was caught up to Paradise where he spoke with Jesus.

1 Corinthians 9:1—Am I (Paul) not as free as anyone else? Am I not an apostle? Haven't I seen Jesus our Lord with my own eyes? Isn't it because of my work that you belong to the Lord?

Acts 9:17—So Ananias went and found Saul. He laid his hands on him and said, "Brother Saul, the Lord Jesus, who appeared to you on the road, has sent me so that you might regain your sight and be filled with the Holy Spirit."

Acts 9:27—Then Barnabas brought him to the apostles and told them how Saul had seen the Lord on the way to Damascus and how the Lord had spoken to Saul. He also told them that Saul had preached boldly in the name of Jesus in Damascus.

Galatians 1:11–12—Dear brothers and sisters, I want you to understand that the gospel message I preach is not based on mere human reasoning. I received my message from no human source, and no one taught me. Instead, I received it by direct revelation from Jesus Christ.

-Stephen's Vision of Heaven-

Stephen is the first Christian martyr recorded in the Bible. He taught that all who proclaimed the gospel of Jesus should be an image of Jesus in the way they live their lives. Because Stephen attempted to teach the truth of the Gospel, those that disputed his claims of the divinity of Jesus, secretly persuaded some men to say he was blaspheming both Moses and God.

Stephen was seized and brought before the Jewish Sanhedrin council. Stephen defended himself by telling them the truth as to why God had given the Law. He showed them how they did not keep the law they claimed to revere and to defend. He told them how God sent His prophets to speak of the coming Messiah and that they were guilty of the blood of Jesus, the killing of the Messiah who had come just as the prophets had proclaimed.

> Acts 7:55–57—But Stephen, full of the Holy Spirit, gazed steadily into heaven and saw the glory of God, and he saw Jesus standing in the place of honor at God's right hand. And he told them, "Look, I see the heavens opened and the Son of Man standing in the place of honor at God's right hand!" Then they put their hands over their ears and began shouting. They rushed at him.

They found Stephen guilty of speaking blasphemous things against Moses and God. They dragged him out of the city with the consent and assistance of "Saul" (the Apostle Paul before his conversion) and they stoned him to death.

Stephen stood his ground, knowing he would die for his belief in Christ. The marvelous thing about this event is that God gave Stephen a glimpse of His Glory before he died.

-Jacob's Vision of Heaven-

Jacob's vision of heaven changed his life. He was never the same after his encounter with God. He did not know exactly what he was seeing, but the majesty of his vision was forever embedded in his memory.

Jacob was traveling to the town of Haren when he decided to rest for the night. He fell asleep on the ground with stones for a pillow and heaven came down to him in a vision. As he dreamed, he saw a ladder that set upon the earth and its top stretched into the heavens. On the ladder, angels were ascending and descending between heaven and earth. Jacob knew God was standing above the ladder.

> Genesis 28:10–13—Meanwhile, Jacob left Beersheba and traveled toward Haran. At sundown he arrived at a good place to set up camp and stopped there for the night. Jacob found a stone to rest his head against and

> lay down to sleep. As he slept, he dreamed of a stairway that reached from the earth up to heaven. And he saw the angels of God going up and down the stairway. At the top of the stairway stood the Lord, and he said, "I am the Lord, the God of your grandfather Abraham, and the God of your father, Isaac. The ground you are lying on belongs to you. I am giving it to you and your descendants.

When Jacob woke from his sleep, he knew without doubt that there was a heaven and God resided there. God became preeminent in his life, and everything about Jacob changed. The symbolic significance of the ladder stretching into the heavens became known almost 2000 years later at the onset of Jesus' ministry.

> John 1:51—Then he said, "I (Jesus) tell you the truth, you will all see heaven open and the angels of God going up and down on the Son of Man, the one who is the stairway between heaven and earth.

The ladder which Jacob saw was an archetype of Jesus as the mediator between heaven and earth. Jesus came down to earth so those who would believe in His name would be able to climb that ladder and live with Him in Paredise forever.

A spiritual journey into the world where God lives

-John's Vision of Heaven-

In the book of Revelations, the Apostle John talks about Heaven as a place of unimaginable beauty where God will dwell with his children, and there will be everlasting joy, contentment, and peace.

The Apostle John was in exile on the Isle of Patmos for preaching the Gospel of Christ. Jesus appeared to him in a vision and gave him the Revelation of a new heaven and a new earth. John's vision begins when he looked up and saw a door open in heaven and heard a voice like a trumpet tell him to come up here.

> Revelations 4:1-3—Then as I looked, I saw a door standing open in heaven, and the same voice I had heard before spoke to me like a trumpet blast. The voice said, "Come up here, and I will show you what must happen after this." And instantly I was in the Spirit, and I saw a throne in heaven and someone sitting on it. The one sitting on the throne was as brilliant as gemstones—like jasper and carnelian. And the glow of an emerald circled his throne like a rainbow.

> Revelations 1:13-15—And standing in the middle of the lampstands was someone like the Son of Man. He was wearing a long robe with a gold sash across his chest. His head and his hair were white like wool, as white

> as snow. And his eyes were like flames of fire. His feet were like polished bronze refined in a furnace, and his voice thundered like mighty ocean waves.

The Apostle John, in his out-of-body experience gives us a picture of what it will be like in heaven. John saw a new heaven and a new earth. Death is not the end, but the beginning of a life in the presence of God.

> Revelation 21:1–4—Then I saw a new heaven and a new earth, for the old heaven and the old earth had disappeared. And the sea was also gone. And I saw the holy city, the New Jerusalem, coming down from God out of heaven like a bride beautifully dressed for her husband. I heard a loud shout from the throne, saying, "Look, God's home is now among his people! He will live with them, and they will be his people. God himself will be with them. He will wipe every tear from their eyes, and there will be no more death or sorrow or crying or pain. All these things are gone forever."

John attempted to describe the indescribable. He portrays the new heaven as an entire city of transparent gold. The walls of the new city are precious jewels. The gates are twelve single pearls. The city itself and its streets are pure gold, yet like transparent glass. The light of the city emanated from God's glory.

> Revelation 21:11—It shone with the glory of God and sparkled like a precious stone—like jasper as clear as crystal.

The Tree of Life

In Genesis 3:22 Adam and Eve were put out of the Garden of Eden so they would no longer be able to partake of the "Tree of Life" and live forever. The cross of Jesus is often referred to as the reinstated "Tree of Life" that was lost to Adam and Eve and their future generations. Jesus offers anyone who will follow Him, eternal life in His new heavenly kingdom. John tells us in Revelations that the "Tree of Life" from the Garden of Eden is restored in the Kingdom of God so all of His children will know their life is eternal.

> Revelations 22:1–2—Then the angel showed me a river with the water of life, clear as crystal, flowing from the throne of God and of the Lamb. It flowed down the center of the main street. On each side of the river grew a tree of life, bearing twelve crops of fruit, with a fresh crop each month. The leaves were used for medicine to heal the nations.

> Revelations 2:7—Anyone with ears to hear must listen to the Spirit and understand what he is saying to the churches. To everyone who is victorious I will give fruit from the tree of life in the paradise of God.

Jesus Describes Heaven

According to the Sermon on the Mount (Matthew 5) the Kingdom of Heaven is a place where the people of God will live some day.

> Matthew 13:44-48—The Kingdom of Heaven is like a treasure that a man discovered hidden in a field. In his excitement, he hid it again and sold everything he owned to get enough money to buy the field. "Again, the Kingdom of Heaven is like a merchant on the lookout for choice pearls. When he discovered a pearl of great value, he sold everything he owned and bought it! "Again, the Kingdom of Heaven is like a fishing net that was thrown into the water and caught fish of every kind. When the net was full, they dragged it up onto the shore, sat down, and sorted the good fish into crates, but threw the bad ones away.

> Matthew 18:3-5—Then he said, "I tell you the truth, unless you turn from your sins and

become like little children, you will never get into the Kingdom of Heaven. So anyone who becomes as humble as this little child is the greatest in the Kingdom of Heaven. "And anyone who welcomes a little child like this on my behalf is welcoming me.

John 3:5–6—Jesus replied, "I assure you, no one can enter the Kingdom of God without being born of water (from their mother's womb) and the Spirit. Humans can reproduce only human life, but the Holy Spirit gives birth to spiritual life.

Matthew 6:33—Seek the Kingdom of God above all else, and live righteously, and he will give you everything you need.

The Manifest Glory of God

In the Bible, the highest heaven, where God lives, is never referred to as a physical place. Although God can manifest in a material form (Theophany), He is not limited to one geographical location.

During the exodus of the Israelite people from Egypt, the Glory of God (The Shekinah Glory) would go before them to lead their way. Although God is omnipresent, He has manifested His presence on earth many times within history. This physical manifestation of God's presence is called the Shekinah Glory. The usual titles found in the Scriptures for the Shekinah Glory are the glory of the Lord or the glory of God.

> Exodus 24:16—And the glory (Shekinah Glory) of the LORD settled down on Mount Sinai, and the cloud covered it for six days. On the seventh day the LORD called to Moses from inside the cloud.

> Exodus 40:34—Then the cloud covered the Tabernacle, and the glory (Shekinah Glory) of the LORD filled the Tabernacle.

> 2 Chronicles 7:1—When Solomon finished praying, fire flashed down from heaven and burned up the burnt offerings and sacrifices, and the glorious (Shekinah Glory) presence of the LORD filled the Temple.

> Ezekiel 1:28—All around him was a glowing halo, like a rainbow shining in the clouds on a rainy day. This is what the glory (Shekinah Glory) of the LORD looked like to me. When I saw it, I fell face down on the ground, and I heard someone's voice speaking to me.

> Acts 7:55—But Stephen, full of the Holy Spirit, gazed steadily into heaven and saw the glory (Shekinah Glory) of God, and he saw

Jesus standing in the place of honor at God's right hand.

Luke 2:8–9—That night there were shepherds staying in the fields nearby, guarding their flocks of sheep. Suddenly, an angel of the Lord appeared among them, and the radiance of the Lord's glory (Shekinah Glory) surrounded them. They were terrified.

In the Gospel of John, our Lord Jesus Christ is introduced as the Son of God who dwelt among men. The Lord Jesus was the dwelling place of the glory of God (Shekinah Glory) among men during His earthly sojourn.

John 1:14—So the Word became human and made his home among us. He was full of unfailing love and faithfulness. And we have seen his glory (Shekinah Glory), the glory of the Father's one and only Son.

Hebrews 1:3—The Son radiates God's own glory (Shekinah Glory) and expresses the very character of God, and he sustains everything by the mighty power of his command. When he had cleansed us from our sins, he sat down in the place of honor at the right hand of the majestic God in heaven.

Matthew 17:1–3—Six days later Jesus took Peter and the two brothers, James and John, and led them up a high mountain to be alone. As the men watched, Jesus' appearance was transformed so that his face shone like the sun, and his clothes became as white as light (Shekinah Glory). Suddenly, Moses and Elijah appeared and began talking with Jesus.

2 Corinthians 4:60—For God, who said, "Let there be light in the darkness," has made this light shine in our hearts so we could know the glory of God (Shekinah Glory) that is seen in the face of Jesus Christ. For the Lord is the Spirit, and wherever the Spirit of the Lord is, there is freedom.

2 Corinthians 3:17–18—So all of us who have had that veil removed can see and reflect the glory (Shekinah Glory) of the Lord. And the Lord—who is the Spirit—makes us more and more like him as we are changed into his glorious image.

The Apostle Paul tells us that as Christians we are the Temple of God, and the Spirit of God (the Shekinah Glory) dwells within us.

> 1 Corinthians 3:16—Don't you realize that all of you together are the Temple of God and that the Spirit of God lives in you?

God's people, now under the new covenant of Jesus Christ, are His Temple and His Church and will be with Him forever in heaven.

> Ephesians 2:18–22—Now all of us can come to the Father through the same Holy Spirit because of what Christ has done for us. So now you Gentiles are no longer strangers and foreigners. You are citizens along with all of God's holy people. You are members of God's family. Together, we are his house, built on the foundation of the apostles and the prophets. And the cornerstone is Christ Jesus himself. We are carefully joined together in him, becoming a holy temple for the Lord. Through him you Gentiles are also being made part of this dwelling where God lives by his Spirit.

God's Love—The Highway to Paradise

John 3:16 is the most fervent verse ever written in the Bible to express God's immeasurable love towards His children. It is the culmination of God's Word given through the Laws and the Prophets, where God gives us

His assurance of salvation and eternal life through His Son, Jesus Christ.

> John 3:16—For this is how God loved the world: He gave his one and only Son, so that everyone who believes in him will not perish but have eternal life.

> Colossians 3:1–5
> Since you have been raised to new life with Christ, set your sights on the realities of heaven, where Christ sits in the place of honor at God's right hand. Think about the things of heaven, not the things of earth. For you died to this life, and your real life is hidden with Christ in God. And when Christ, who is your life, is revealed to the whole world, you will share in all his glory. So put to death the sinful, earthly things lurking within you. Have nothing to do with sexual immorality, impurity, lust, and evil desires. Don't be greedy, for a greedy person is an idolater, worshiping the things of this world.

Chapter Nine

Supernatural Dreams and Visions

Job 33:14-15
For God speaks again and again, though people do not recognize it. He speaks in dreams, in visions of the night, when deep sleep falls on people as they lie in their beds.

Joel 2:28–29
"Then, after doing all those things, I will pour out my Spirit upon all people. Your sons and daughters will prophesy. Your old men will dream dreams, and your young men will see visions. In those days I will pour out my Spirit even on servants—men and women alike.

Dreams and Visions

Dreaming is a natural physiological function that is common to every human being and is necessary for maintaining mental and emotional health. While, most of our dreams are of common types, every Christian needs to be aware that sometimes God uses our dreams in a supernatural way.

When to know a dream is from God or when it's just a natural dream may sometimes be difficult to discern. A dream can be a very subjective experience, but most of us recognize that a supernatural dream far exceeds a normal dream. The supernatural dream is usually easily remembered, our emotions are strongly affected, and we have the feeling we have somehow transcended the natural world.

Dreams and Visions Throughout History

Dreams and their interpretation have been a central theme of many cultures throughout recorded history. The earliest known recorded dreams came from the ancient land of Mesopotamia. They were written on clay tablets that date back to around 3100 BC. According to these early records, the Mesopotamians believed that not only could they receive prophecies (a divinely inspired word or a revealed meaning) from the spiritual world, but the spirit would leave the body during sleep and visit other worldly places.

During the Egyptian, Greek, and Roman periods, spiritual dreams were highly revered as divine messages from their deities. Dreams written down on papyrus in ancient Egypt were dated as far back as 2000 BC. During this era sacred places were set up specifically to induce (incubate) dreams that would bring a message from the spiritual world to the dreamer. After due ritual preparation, their deity would appear and deliver a divine message. Dream interpretation was big business in the ancient world. Since spiritual dreams were deemed to be from the divine, most often an astrologer or priest was considered to be the most worthy to perform the interpretation. Even kings would seek out dream specialists and some kept many within their court.

Dreams were an extension of ancient's daily lives. They believed dreams spoke to them about issues in their life that needed attention, could help them solve problems, allow them to see into the future, and could heal them from diseases.

Interpreting Dreams and Visions

The Bible contains many dreams of divine significance given to privileged and common people alike. The meaning of a divine message was sometimes obvious and unmistakable. At other times, the message was symbolic, and a dream specialist (Oneiromancer) was used to unfold the meaning.

- A spiritual dream given to Abimelech was obvious as to its meaning.

  Genesis 20:3–7—But that night God came to Abimelech in a dream and told him, "You are a dead man, for that woman you have taken is already married!" But Abimelech had not slept with her yet, so he said, "Lord, will you destroy an innocent nation? Didn't Abraham tell me, 'She is my sister'? And she herself said, 'Yes, he is my brother.' I acted in complete innocence! My hands are clean." In the dream God responded, "Yes, I know you are innocent. That's why I kept you from sinning against me, and why I did not let you touch her. Now return the woman to her husband, and he will pray for you, for he is a prophet. Then you will live. But if you don't return her to him, you can be sure that you and all your people will die."

- A symbolic spiritual dream given to King Nebuchadnezzar.

Daniel 2:31-36—"In your vision, Your Majesty, you saw standing before you a huge, shining statue of a man. It was a frightening sight. The head of the statue was made of fine gold. Its chest and arms were silver, its belly and thighs were bronze, its legs were iron, and its feet were a combination of iron and baked clay. As you watched, a rock was cut from a mountain, but not by human hands. It struck the feet of iron and clay, smashing them to bits. The whole statue was crushed into small pieces of iron, clay, bronze, silver, and gold.

Then the wind blew them away without a trace, like chaff on a threshing floor. But the rock that knocked the statue down became a great mountain that covered the whole earth. "That was the dream. Now we will tell the king what it means.

- Daniel interprets Nebuchadnezzar's symbolic dream.

Daniel 2:39–45—"But after your kingdom comes to an end, another kingdom, inferior to yours, will rise to take your place. After that kingdom has fallen, yet a third kingdom, represented by bronze, will rise to rule the world. Following that kingdom, there will be a fourth one, as strong as iron. That kingdom will smash and crush all previous empires, just as iron smashes and crushes everything it strikes. The feet and toes you saw were a combination of iron and baked clay, showing that this kingdom will be divided. Like iron mixed with clay, it will have some of the strength of iron. But while some parts of it will be as strong as iron, other parts will be as weak as clay. This mixture of iron and clay also shows that these kingdoms will try to strengthen themselves by forming alliances with each other through intermarriage. But they will not hold together, just as iron and clay do not mix.

"During the reigns of those kings, the God of heaven will set up a kingdom that will never be destroyed or conquered. It will crush all these kingdoms into nothingness, and it will stand forever. That is the meaning of the rock cut from the mountain, though not by human hands, that crushed to pieces the statue of iron, bronze, clay, silver, and gold. The great God was showing the king what will happen in the future. The dream is true, and its meaning is certain."

Types of Spiritual Visions

- Open mind vision.

An open mind vision is one that is seen by our physical eyes while awake. The senses perceive some object that otherwise would be invisible. This is a supernatural appearance of a person or thing which is called an apparition.

2 Kings 6:17—Then Elisha prayed, "O LORD, open his eyes and let him see!" The LORD opened the young man's eyes, and when he looked up, he saw that the hillside around Elisha was filled with horses and chariots of fire.

The transfiguration of Jesus is another good example of this kind of vision. Here the Apostles Peter, James, and John see Moses and Elijah talking with Jesus. All three appear to the apostles to be quite real. But Jesus tells them that what they had just seen was a "vision."

Matthew 17:9—As they went back down the mountain, Jesus commanded them, "Don't tell anyone what you have seen until the Son of Man has been raised from the dead."

- Trance vision.

A trance vision is defined as a mental state where our waking consciousness is suspended. The word "trance" literally means to stand outside yourself or to be put outside of your normal state of mind. Daydreams are considered trance visions.

Acts 10:9–12—The next day as Cornelius's messengers were nearing the town, Peter went up on the flat roof to pray. It was about noon, and he was hungry. But while a meal was being prepared, he fell into a trance. He saw the sky open, and something like a large sheet was let down by its four corners. In the sheet were all sorts of animals, reptiles, and birds.

- Hypnagogic vision.

    A hypnagogic vision is when one hears a voice or sees a vivid scene while in the state just before falling completely asleep.

    1 Samuel 3:3–5—The lamp of God had not yet gone out, and Samuel was sleeping in the Tabernacle) near the Ark of God. Suddenly the Lord called out, "Samuel!" "Yes?" Samuel replied. "What is it?" He got up and ran to Eli. "Here I am. Did you call me?" "I didn't call you," Eli replied. "Go back to bed." So he did.

- Night vision.

    A night vision is a spiritual vision that occurs while dreaming. Night visions can be straight forward or may contain symbolism. The Bible also describes night visions that involve clairvoyance (seeing future events) and precognition (extrasensory perception of future events).

    Acts 16:9—That night Paul had a vision: A man from Macedonia in northern Greece was standing there, pleading with him, "Come over to Macedonia and help us!"

    Matthew 1:20—As he considered this, an angel of the Lord appeared to him in a dream. "Joseph, son of David," the angel said, "do not be afraid to take Mary as your wife. For the child within her was conceived by the Holy Spirit.

Genesis 37:5–7—One night Joseph had a dream, and when he told his brothers about it, they hated him more than ever. "Listen to this dream," he said. "We were out in the field, tying up bundles of grain. Suddenly my bundle stood up, and your bundles all gathered around and bowed low before mine!"

Daniel 7:13—As my vision continued that night, I saw someone like a son of man coming with the clouds of heaven. He approached the Ancient One and was led into his presence.

- Audible Vision.

An audible vision is a message that is heard rather than seen.

Acts 18:9—One night the Lord spoke to Paul in a vision and told him, "Don't be afraid! Speak out! Don't be silent!"

Genesis 15:1—Some time later, the Lord spoke to Abram in a vision and said to him,

"Do not be afraid, Abram, for I will protect you, and your reward will be great."

God's Purpose for Spiritual Dreams and Visions

Today, Christians are awakening to their natural ability to hear from God. God is speaking to them during the quiet time of their spirit, during meditation, or in a dream when the outside world is left behind and it is impossible to ignore Him.

> 2 Peter 1:20–21—Above all, you must realize that no prophecy in Scripture ever came from the prophet's own understanding, or from human initiative. No, those prophets were moved by the Holy Spirit, and they spoke from God.

Dreams (night visions) are one of the most overlooked forms of communication used by God. The Bible consistently reveals God as speaking to His children through this universal phenomenon. Yet, today dreams tend to be ignored. God uses dreams in many different ways:

A spiritual journey into the world where God lives

- To reveal His plans.

    Matthew 1:20—As he considered this, an angel of the Lord appeared to him in a dream. "Joseph, son of David," the angel said, "do not be afraid to take Mary as your wife. For the child within her was conceived by the Holy Spirit.

- To correct.

    Job 33:14–18—For God speaks again and again, though people do not recognize it. He speaks in dreams, in visions of the night, when deep sleep falls on people as they lie in their beds. He whispers in their ears and terrifies them with warnings. He makes them turn from doing wrong; he keeps them from pride. He protects them from the grave, from crossing over the river of death.

- To guide.

    Genesis 46:2–3—During the night God spoke to him in a vision. "Jacob! Jacob!" he called. "Here I am," Jacob replied. "I am God, the God of your father," the voice said. "Do not be afraid to go down to Egypt, for there I will make your family into a great nation.

- To encourage, edify, and comfort.

  Acts 18:9–10—One night the Lord spoke to Paul in a vision and told him, "Don't be afraid! Speak out! Don't be silent! For I am with you, and no one will attack and harm you, for many people in this city belong to me."

- To reveal the future.

  Isaiah 2:1–2—This is a vision that Isaiah son of Amoz saw concerning Judah and Jerusalem: In the last days, the mountain of the Lord's house will be the highest of all—the most important place on earth. It will be raised above the other hills, and people from all over the world will stream there to worship.

- To give a warning.

  Matthew 2:12—When it was time to leave, they returned to their own country by another route, for God had warned them in a dream not to return to Herod.

  Genesis 31:24—But the previous night God had appeared to Laban the Aramean in a dream and told him, "I'm warning you-leave Jacob alone!"

- To instruct.

    Psalms 16:7—I will bless the LORD who guides me; even at night my heart instructs me.

- To reveal His will.

    Genesis 28:12–13—As he slept, he dreamed of a stairway that reached from the earth up to heaven. And he saw the angels of God going up and down the stairway. At the top of the stairway stood the Lord, and he said, "I am the Lord, the God of your grandfather Abraham, and the God of your father, Isaac. The ground you are lying on belongs to you. I am giving it to you and your descendants."

- To protect.

    Genesis 15:1—Some time later, the LORD spoke to Abram in a vision and said to him, "Do not be afraid, Abram, for I will protect you, and your reward will be great."

- To reveal a mystery.

    Daniel 2:28—But there is a God in heaven who reveals secrets, and he has shown King Nebuchadnezzar what will happen in the future. Now I will tell you your dream and the visions you saw as you lay on your bed.

- To answer petitions and prayers.

    1 Kings 3:5—That night the LORD appeared to Solomon in a dream, and God said, "What do you want? Ask, and I will give it to you!"

- To reveal destinies.

    Amos 8:1-3—Then the Sovereign LORD showed me another vision. In it I saw a basket filled with ripe fruit. "What do you see, Amos?" he asked. I replied, "A basket full of ripe fruit." Then the LORD said, "Like this fruit, Israel is ripe for punishment! I will not delay their punishment again. In that day the singing in the temple will turn to wailing. Dead bodies will be scattered everywhere. They will be carried out of the city in silence. I, the Sovereign LORD, have spoken!"

Bible Prophets versus Seers

In the Bible, from Genesis to Revelations, God spoke to His people through prophets and seers.

Numbers 12:6—And the Lord said to them, "Now listen to what I say: "If there were prophets among you, I, the Lord, would reveal myself in visions. I would speak to them in dreams.

Many theologians believe there is a distinct difference between a biblical prophet and a biblical seer. A prophet is one who receives a word of knowledge. A Seer is a prophet who also sees visions. Although the Hebrew words for "Prophet" and "Seer" are different, they are at times used interchangeably in the Bible.

Iddo, Son of Zechariah, was called a seer simply because he had visions, as opposed to Nathan, who was a prophet, but not a seer.

> 2 Chronicles 9:29—The rest of the events of Solomon's reign, from beginning to end, are recorded in The Record of Nathan the Prophet, and The Prophecy of Ahijah from Shiloh, and also in The Visions of Iddo the Seer, concerning Jeroboam son of Nebat.

In the New Testament, a prophet is one who receives a word of knowledge and may also see visions. Look at the prophetic and revelatory vision given to John in the book of Revelations.

> Revelations 1:9–11—I, John, am your brother and your partner in suffering and in God's Kingdom and in the patient endurance to which Jesus calls us. I was exiled to the island

of Patmos for preaching the Word of God and for my testimony about Jesus. It was the Lord's Day, and I was worshiping in the Spirit. Suddenly, I heard behind me a loud voice like a trumpet blast. It said, "Write in a book everything you see, and send it to the seven churches in the cities of Ephesus, Smyrna, Pergamum, Thyatira, Sardis, Philadelphia, and Laodicea."

Elisha's Spiritual Sight

In 2 Kings, the Word of God gives us a glimpse of Elisha's spiritual sight. Elisha could not only see in the natural world he also had the ability to see into the spiritual world. While Elisha was able to perceive situations in the spiritual world, his servant perceived things only in the natural. Because Elisha's servant was only able to see in the natural world, he was in fear of King Aram's army.

King Aram did not know how the Lord was using the prophet Elisha to expose his military plans. So, he sent horses and chariots and a great army to surround the place where Elisha and his servant were staying. When Elisha's servant saw the army encamped around them, he became afraid.

> 2 Kings 6:15–17—When the servant of the man of God got up early the next morning and went outside, there were troops, horses, and chariots everywhere. "Oh, sir, what will

we do now?" the young man cried to Elisha. "Don't be afraid!" Elisha told him. "For there are more on our side than on theirs!" Then Elisha prayed, "O LORD, open his eyes and let him see!" The LORD opened the young man's eyes, and when he looked up, he saw that the hillside around Elisha was filled with horses and chariots of fire.

Elisha prayed for his servant's spiritual eyes to be opened so that he could see into the spiritual world and know what was really happening around them. The Lord responded to Elisha's prayer of faith, and his servant was able to see the horses and chariots of fire. Elisha's servant was able to see what Elisha was seeing through the power of the Holy Spirit.

Spiritual visions were common among our Church Fathers

The following are only a few examples to show how our Church Fathers understood spiritual dreams and visions.

- Polycarp (69—155), bishop or overseer of Smyrna.

  Polycarp was a student of the Apostle John and others who had personally sat under the teaching of Jesus, connecting him to both Jesus' disciples and to the beginning age of the Church Fathers. While Christians were under the persecution of the Roman Emperor Marcus Aurelius, the Lord revealed to Polycarp that he would be burned at the stake. While in a dream he saw the pillow under his head caught fire and realized that this image signified his impending death.

- Irenaeus (120—200), Bishop or Overseer of Lyons.

Irenaeus was acquainted with Polycarp in his early years. He believed that although God is invisible, He gives us visions and dreams through which He brings to us the likeness of His nature and glory.

- Origen (185—254), Scholar and Christian theologian.

Origen believed in the universal salvation and was the first known theologian to describe the route the soul followed on its way to heaven.

- Augustine (354—430) Bishop of North Africa.

Augustine believed that both angels and demons have direct contact with the human mind and can send messages to the inner eye, while awake or asleep.

If spiritual visions were so important to early Christians and our Church Fathers, why are spiritual visions not seen as important to Christians today?

Anyone wanting to know more about the dreams and visions of the early Church Fathers will find the book "Communicating With God" by Mark and Patti Virkler an interesting and informative read.

Most Dreams are of Natural Origin

The majority of our dreams are of natural origin. This is our mind working through our daily activities or unresolved subconscious issues. These dreams should be monitored to determine if there is some issue in our lives that need attention. Be aware that Satan, the enemy of our souls, is not ignorant of the power of dreams. A dream from God will never go against His Holy Word.

> Ecclesiastes 5:3—Too much activity gives you restless dreams; too many words make you a fool.

> Isaiah 29:8—A hungry person dreams of eating, but wakes up still hungry. A thirsty person dreams of drinking, but is still faint from thirst when morning comes. So it will be with your enemies, with those who attack Mount Zion."

> Isaiah 56:10—For the leaders of my people—the LORD's watchmen, his shepherds—are blind and ignorant. They are like silent watchdogs that give no warning when danger comes. They love to lie around, sleeping and dreaming.

The Gift of Spiritual Sight

Today, our churches are opening their eyes to the gift of spiritual sight because of the many Christians who are now experiencing the gift of seeing into the spiritual world.

I have talked with many Christians who believe they have received a spiritual vision from God at least one time in their lives. I have also talked with Christians who say they receive spiritual visions on a regular basis, but are afraid to say anything. They find their spiritual visions to be neither unbiblical nor anti-biblical.

> Acts 2:17—In the last days,' God says, 'I will pour out my Spirit upon all people. Your sons and daughters will prophesy. Your young men will see visions, and your old men will dream dreams.'

My wife and I have a wonderful Christian friend who has had the gift of spiritual sight as far back as she can remember. Her gifts include empathy, premonition and precognition dreams, clairvoyance or second sight, and surreal night visions of other worlds. What is unusual about her is that she does not want these gifts, mainly because of the stigma that goes along with them and the negative impact people have had on her life. I asked if I could use a couple of her precognitive dreams in my book and was quite surprised when she said "yes,"

Letter from a friend named Amy.

> I have had many precognitive dreams throughout my life, and they still continue to happen on a regular basis.
>
> I have found over the years that it doesn't need to be just anyone close to me. It is also major events. I'm sure I have had experiences and not connected them to anything or anyone. Sometimes I ignore them and other times I'm on the phone calling everyone I know to see if they are ok. I love to dream, but, sometimes I wonder if it is a blessing or a curse. The dream always feels real, as though I am there when it happens. I can see, feel, hear, and smell. When I have a dream I'm not too sure about, all I can do is sit and wait to see what happens. You cannot tell anyone, you cannot try to stop them. People either don't believe you or they think you're crazy. You also don't want to mess up what is supposed to happen. God has it all written down already and who am I to intervene no matter how much I would like to.

Supernatural Dreams and Visions

The Day My Daddy Died.

I was eight years old, and while getting ready for bed, my father told me he was going deer hunting in the morning. I said my good night, that I loved him, and went to bed. My father was an avid hunter. He was always deer hunting, duck hunting, even hunting wild boar. I knew he was going early in the morning to deer hunt. In the middle of the night, I had my first experience of true fear. I was eight years old.

I had a dream, I was standing all alone in the middle of the woods, I was in my long pink night gown and it was dark and cold. I could see the shadows of a very tall, thin trees surrounding me. All of a sudden hundreds of deer came charging at me. In the distance, I saw my dad. I heard him scream! The deer had trampled him. Then he was just gone.

I woke up looking to find my daddy, but he had already left. I started to cry and told my momma that my daddy was dead. She tried to console me, thinking it was just a nightmare. This was just another hunting excursion for my father. We had breakfast and got ready to go to the neighbor's house down the road. My momma opened up the door, and we were half way down the walk when the police pulled up.

A spiritual journey into the world where God lives

I remember them looking at her and asked if she had any family or friends to call. I looked up at the policeman and said "my daddy is dead, isn't he?" He just looked at me and told me to go to my room. I slowly walked down the hall, turned into my room, and grabbed my little monkey named Herbie that my daddy had bought me. I remember just sitting there crying going "my daddy is dead" over and over again while rocking back and forth.

My father was shot by a friend 100 yards away with all reflective gear on. He said he thought he was a deer.

Explosion in the Sky.

When I was sixteen, in my dream, it was a really sunny clear day. It was humid and very hot out. All of a sudden I saw a massive explosion in the sky with trails of smoke going in several directions. I woke up in a cold sweat and felt really sick. I know now I tend to feel sick when my dreams are real. The TV was on when I went downstairs to call off from work. I picked up the phone and started dialing while watching the TV. There it was on TV, exactly what happened in my dream. I became disoriented and started crying and yelling. There it was the explosion of the Space Shuttle Challenger!

Supernatural Dreams and Visions

Seeing Into God's World

Dream induction and dream interpretation techniques are on the rise. Many books can be found in just about any bookstore on the subject. Day and night visions are today finally opening the veil to the spiritual world.

Spiritual visions coming to people in our current age need to be recognized as important. Christians need to wake up (or go to sleep as the case may be) and pay more attention to their night visions. We are experiencing an overlapping of realities at this time. And as we come closer to the End of Days our dreams and visions are taking on a more significant and prominent role in Christian life. Until our dreams are seen as a powerful way to view and understand the spiritual world, we will not be able to receive all of the awesome knowledge and wonders God has waiting for us.

Most Christians today believe reality to be the concrete world they live in. What if I told you the world we live in is only a fraction of a larger reality you can be a part of? Let's say there is a place across the street from where you live and that people of an earlier time considered to be sacred. They went there to hear from God. But today very few people go there because it is seen as a myth that has no meaning in today's world. Then a friend that decided to visit there told you the most awesome stories about what you could do there and it is free to anyone who wishes to enter.

Some of the things your friend told you that were possible there:

A spiritual journey into the world where God lives

- Learn about your deepest fears.
- Learn about areas of your life that need attention.
- See future events.
- Learn about your nightmares.
- Communicate with God.
- Communicate with angels.
- Visit and navigate worlds that are beyond imagination.
- Gain a much clearer understanding of God's glory and love.
- Receive answers to your most intimate questions.
- Receive inspiration for things that interests you.
- Fly over rivers, mountains, and forests.
- Know that you are always loved and will never be alone.
- Let go of the past and live in the present moment.
- Be in a place you believe only God could create just for you.

Would you not want to visit there? I would. Ask God to visit you in your dreams. Maybe He is already there.

Colossians 3:1–4
Since you have been raised to new life with Christ, set your sights on the realities of

heaven, where Christ sits in the place of honor at God's right hand. Think about the things of heaven, not the things of earth. For you died to this life, and your real life is hidden with Christ in God. And when Christ, who is your life, is revealed to the whole world, you will share in all his glory.

Chapter Ten

God's Lost Communication

Job 33:14-16
"But you are wrong, and I will show you why. For God is greater than any human being. So why are you bringing a charge against him? Why say he does not respond to people's complaints? For God speaks again and again, though people do not recognize it. He speaks in dreams, in visions of the night, when deep sleep falls on people as they lie in their beds.

The Last Days

Jesus prophesied that before this world will end, His gospel of truth "the Good News about the Kingdom" will be preached to all the world. He tells us that when this prophecy is fulfilled, "The End of Days" will come.

The world today is fast becoming polarized into two camps—those who serve the one true God, and those who serve their self. Scripture refers to these two camps as the believers and the unbelievers, the sheep and the goats, the wheat and weeds (tares).

> Matthew 24:1–14—Later, Jesus sat on the Mount of Olives. His disciples came to him privately and said, "Tell us, when will all this happen? What sign will signal your return and the end of the world?" Jesus told them, "Don't let anyone mislead you, for many will come in my name, claiming, 'I am the Messiah.' They will deceive many. And you will hear of wars and threats of wars, but don't panic. Yes, these things must take place, but the end won't follow immediately. Nation will go to war against nation, and kingdom against kingdom. There will be famines and earthquakes in many parts of the world. But all this is only the first of the birth pains, with more to come. "Then you will be arrested, persecuted, and killed. You will be hated all over the world because you are my followers. And many will turn away from me and betray and hate each other. And many false prophets will appear and will deceive many people. Sin will be rampant everywhere, and the love of many will grow cold. But the one who endures to the end will be saved. And

the Good News about the Kingdom will be preached throughout the whole world, so that all nations will hear it and then the end will come.

When we refer to the last days, we are talking about the age of the Church, which started when Jesus was baptized into His ministry and will culminate when He returns.

Peter, exercising the gift of prophecy during the time of Pentecost (the Jewish Feast of Weeks) stood up and told the people that we are now in the last days about which the prophet Joel spoke about. Peter's message clearly defines for us the New Testament meaning of the term "Last Days."

> Acts 2:17–18—(Peter referring to Joel's prophecy) 'In the last days,' God says, 'I will pour out my Spirit upon all people. Your sons and daughters will prophesy. Your young men will see visions, and your old men will dream dreams. In those days I will pour out my Spirit even on my servants—men and women alike—and they will prophesy. And I will cause wonders in the heavens above and signs on the earth below—blood and fire and clouds of smoke. The sun will become dark, and the moon will turn blood red before that great and glorious day of the LORD arrives.

It has been in the climate of Pentecost (the last days) that we have seen the rise of what many call spiritual enlightenment. Those who exercise the God-given powers that Jesus said we would have.

During Pentecost all the disciples were meeting together in one place when the spiritual world opened and crossed the veil into the physical realm.

> Acts 2:1–4—On the day of Pentecost all the believers were meeting together in one place. Suddenly, there was a sound from heaven like the roaring of a mighty windstorm, and it filled the house where they were sitting. Then, what looked like flames or tongues of fire appeared and settled on each of them. And everyone present was filled with the Holy Spirit and began speaking in other languages, as the Holy Spirit gave them this ability.

The outpouring of spiritual abilities in the last days is given to Christians to fulfill the mission of the Church. Paul tells us in his letter to the Corinthian that we will have every spiritual power (gift) we need to serve our Lord and Savior—Jesus Christ.

> 1 Corinthians 1:7–11—Now you have every spiritual gift you need as you eagerly wait for the return of our Lord Jesus Christ. He will keep you strong to the end so that you will be free from all blame on the day when our

Lord Jesus Christ returns. God will do this, for he is faithful to do what he says, and he has invited you into partnership with his Son, Jesus Christ our Lord. I appeal to you, dear brothers and sisters, by the authority of our Lord Jesus Christ, to live in harmony with each other. Let there be no divisions in the church. Rather, be of one mind, united in thought and purpose. For some members of Chloe's household have told me about your quarrels, my dear brothers and sisters.

1 Peter 4:8–11—Most important of all, continue to show deep love for each other, for love covers a multitude of sins. Cheerfully share your home with those who need a meal or a place to stay. God has given each of you a gift from his great variety of spiritual gifts. Use them well to serve one another. Do you have the gift of speaking? Then speak as though God himself were speaking through you. Do you have the gift of helping others? Do it with all the strength and energy that God supplies. Then everything you do will bring glory to God through Jesus Christ. All glory and power to him forever and ever! Amen.

Dr. Rice's Book "We Can Have Revival Now."

Here in "these last days" is used of the time in which Jesus Christ brought God's revelation to earth in person, when He walked on earth. In the ministry of Jesus Christ, then, began the period of time called "these last days." The period properly means the whole age, we suppose, as defined by Joel, and the period certainly began with Jesus Christ (p. 75).

Paul spoke of the end of the last days in his letter to Timothy.

> 2 Timothy 3:1–6—You should know this, Timothy, that in the last days there will be very difficult times. For people will love only themselves and their money. They will be boastful and proud, scoffing at God, disobedient to their parents, and ungrateful. They will consider nothing sacred. They will be unloving and unforgiving they will slander others and have no self-control. They will be cruel and hate what is good. They will betray their friends, be reckless, be puffed up with pride, and love pleasure rather than God. They will act religious, but they will reject the power that could make them godly. Stay away from people like that! They are the kind who work their way into people's homes and win the confidence of vulnerable women who are

burdened with the guilt of sin and controlled by various desires.

Believers are discovering latent spiritual talents and powers within them. We have seen many begin to literally harness the power of the mind. We have seen a rise in spiritual knowledge and understanding not thought possible. The veil between the physical world and the world of the supernatural is getting shorter as we get closer to the return of Christ. We must be able to sift and sort through what is Spiritual Truth and what is Satan's Counterfeit. God will give us discernment, if we only ask Him.

Satan always tries to imitate God's powers. He knew God would be pouring out His Spirit in the last days, so he sent his minions to counterfeit God's spiritual outpouring and to intimidate Christians with his demonic powers. In the last couple of centuries, we have seen the rise of the occult, witchcraft, Quija boards, séances, devil worship and false prophets. Satan wants to counterfeit the awakening of the Holy Spirit in God's people.

With the moral decline of the world and the growing animosity towards God, Christians, and the Bible, we need to be open to all forms of godly communication. Sadly, many churches today disregard dreams and visions as insignificant and unimportant to the body of Christ. I believe they do so at the loss of God's best for the Church. God wants us to use them in the Church to edify, exhort, and comfort His people. He wants to encourage us to trust in Him, live by His Word, and rejoice in the hope of His return.

In the midst of all of this, God is speaking to many people around the world through dreams and visions, giving them the opportunity to know Him while His forgiveness and mercy can still be found. Make no mistake the world is in a downward spiral. God's end-day-plan is right on track.

Supernatural Dreams and Visions are Other Worldly Adventures?

We can wake up from a dream feeling joyful and calm or wake up sweating and feeling intense fear. Our bodies react to some dreams as though they are real. This begs the question, are some dreams actually real? Yes! I believe some dreams are just as real, if not more real, than waking life.

My curiosity about the dream world began when I was researching the meaning of symbols in biblical visions and dreams. As I studied biblical symbolism, I began to understand just how important dreams and visions were to God as a way of communicating His divine will to His people.

The first dream interpretation that caught my attention was the narrative of Nathanael where Jesus revealed the symbolism in Jacob's dream.

Jacob, with his mother's help, stole Esau's firstborn inheritance. Jacob then fled the land because of Esau's hateful desire to kill him. On his journey, Jacob had his famous dream of a staircase that stretched from earth to heaven on which angels ascended and descended. Jacob saw a stairway extending from heaven to earth.

> Genesis 28:10:13—Jacob left Beersheba and set out for Harran. When he reached a certain place, he stopped for the night because the sun had set. Taking one of the stones there, he put it under his head and lay down to sleep. He had a dream in which he saw a stairway resting on the earth, with its top reaching to heaven, and the angels of God were ascending and descending on it. There above it stood the LORD, and he said: "I am the LORD, the God of your father Abraham and the God of Isaac. I will give you and your descendants the land on which you are lying.

Jesus later claimed to be the ladder in the dream Jacob had over two thousand years earlier. Jesus revealed that He is the intercessor between heaven and the physical realm (staircase descending and ascending from heaven to earth).

> John 1:51—Then he said, "I tell you the truth, you will all see heaven open and the angels of God going up and down on the Son of Man, the one who is the stairway between heaven and earth.

This scripture shows God, in His infinite love reaching down from heaven to His children. Jesus is the stairway that spans the veil between God and Man. The message of Jesus is simply this:

> John 14:6—Jesus told him, "I am the way, the truth, and the life. No one can come to the Father except through me.

The symbolic interpretation of Jacob's Staircase by Jesus was an awakening moment for me, "Does God still communicate with His people today through dreams and visions?" I knew that I needed to dig deeper into God's lost communication—the world of dreams and visions.

Since dreams have been an important part of all cultures throughout history; I wanted to know why dreams are not seen as important today? Or are they? And we just ignore them.

Do People Today Have Spiritual Dreams and Visions?

Spiritual dreams, spiritual visions, and spiritual gifts were given throughout biblical history for the purpose of bringing glory to God and the light of Christ out of the Church and into the world.

Throughout Church history and in modern times, many churches do believe that God speaks to us in the form of spiritual dreams and visions. Christian churches that teach this include Catholic, Pentecostal, and Charismatic.

> Numbers 12:6—"If there were prophets among you, I, the Lord, would reveal myself in visions. I would speak to them in dreams.

Know that many believers in the Church are naturally gifted. Have you ever known someone who was naturally gifted? My brother is a talented marine artist. He has never had an art lesson, yet his paintings are so beautiful and realistic they sell for thousands of dollars. Not everyone is blessed in this way, but we can all create paintings.

It is the same with spiritual gifts. We are not all prophets, but we can all prophesy. We are not all healers, but we can all heal. We are not all seers, but we can all see. We are not all called to be Pastors, however, all of us are called to be God's ministers to a fallen world. We are all called to share the gospel of Jesus Christ. God gives every one of us the right gift at the right time to do His work as long as it is for His glory (brings the light of Jesus into the world).

When someone has a unique talent or special gift given to him or her by God for the Church, it is called a charge or an office. This person knows, without doubt, the call to this charge was from God. It is easy to see these gifts in a Spirit filled Church.

Genesis to Revelations—God Spoke to People Through Dreams and Visions

The Bible has many scriptures that speak to us of dreams and visions where the spiritual world is seen. Spiritual visions that come during the day are referred to as trance visions. Spiritual dreams that come to us during the night while we are asleep are referred to as night visions.

We can choose to invite God's Holy Spirit to open our eyes to the spiritual world through dreams and visions or we can just ignore it. Just as the prophets and visionaries of old, as believers, we are all able to have spiritual dreams and visions.

God has not limited us to know Him only in His Word or by His spirit. We can see His work in the world around us and we can see into His world. If we put on our spiritual lenses, there is no place we will not be able to see God.

- A Holy Man whose eyes are open to the spiritual world can open the eyes of another.

    2 Kings 6:17—Then Elisha prayed, "O LORD, open his eyes and let him see!" The LORD opened the young man's eyes, and when he looked up, he saw that the hillside around Elisha was filled with horses and chariots of fire.

- In times of trouble, God may come to us in a vision.

  Ezekiel 1:1—On July 31 of my thirtieth year, while I was with the Judean exiles beside the Kebar River in Babylon, the heavens were opened and I saw visions of God.

- Early Christians had what are today called out-of-body experiences.

  2 Corinthians 12:2—I was caught up to the third heaven fourteen years ago. Whether I was in my body or out of my body, I don't know—only God knows.

  Revelations 4:1—Then, as I looked, I saw a door standing open in heaven, and the same voice I had heard before spoke to me like a trumpet blast. The voice said, "Come up here, and I will show you what must happen after this."

- God can use a prophet or a dream to reveal Himself.

  Deuteronomy 13:1–3—"Suppose there are prophets among you, or those who dream dreams about the future, and they promise you signs or miracles, and the predicted signs or miracles occur. If they then say, 'Come, let us worship other gods'—gods you have not known before—do not listen to them. The LORD your God is testing you to see if you truly love him with all your heart and soul.

- Secrets are revealed in night visions.

    Daniel 2:19—That night the secret was revealed to Daniel in a vision. Then Daniel praised the God of heaven.

I found it inspiring to research biblical dreams and visions because I know God is immutable (does not change) and reveals Himself today the same as He did in ancient times.

God Speaks Through the Silence of Our Minds

If we can accept that God speaks to us through dreams and visions, we can then see the reasons why. When we are awake, we filter everything through the mind that corresponds to the human experience. Spiritual dreams and visions bypass our mind and come to the forefront when we are sleeping or when our conscious mind goes into the background. God uses this medium of revelation to cut through agendas of the mind that can cause us to miss out on the valuable things He wants us to know. God continues today to use dreams and visions as one of the most common ways He communicates with His children.

The dreams and visions that come from God are usually very spiritual experiences and their insights are not easily forgotten. They become a part of the heart and mind of the person receiving them. Our dreams and visions can be filled with supernatural adventures and at times prophetic insight.

God uses our dreams and visions to edify, encourage, comfort, answer a question, or chasten us if needed. He may even give us a prophecy or take us on a tour of His world. Spiritual visions can occur when we quiet our mind, lay back, close our eyes and just meditate on the awesome grace of God.

> Psalm 46:10—"Be still, and know that I am God"

Being Spiritually Aware

The first step in developing our spiritual eyes is being spiritually aware. The spiritual world is in us and all around us, but we must take the time to see. Stillness of mind is a major key factor. We cannot hear from or see into the spiritual world if we are preoccupied with anything in the natural world.

> Luke 17:20-21—One day the Pharisees asked Jesus, "When will the Kingdom of God come?" Jesus replied, "The Kingdom of God

can't be detected by visible signs. You won't be able to say, 'Here it is!' or 'It's over there!' For the Kingdom of God is already among you (in and around you)."

We as believers have a right to seek and hear from the spiritual world. We should expect divine visitations where the Lord, His angels and His world opens to us.

John 14:21—Those who accept my commandments and obey them are the ones who love me. And because they love me, my Father will love them. And I will love them and reveal myself to each of them."

Dream Symbolism

Most of our nighttime dreams are very elusive. If they are not written down or an effort is not made to remember them, they quickly fade. By the time we are dressed and ready for the day our dreams have usually faded into oblivion. Only dreams that are vivid enough to capture our waking consciousness are remembered for any length of time. I believe God paints our spiritual night visions in a way that will get our conscious attention.

God communicated more frequently with people in the Bible by night visions (spiritual dreams) than any other type. Many of these night visions seemed absurd, yet when interpreted were quite meaningful.

One example is Pharaoh's dream, as recorded in Genesis 41:17–32. He saw seven fat cows and seven lean cows, seven good ears of corn and seven bad ears of corn. The meaning of the dream became clear when it was interpreted by the prophet Daniel.

Daniel, interpreting the dream, said that after seven good years there would come a time when a lack of rain would cause a great seven year famine to cover the land. Daniel had the people store more than enough grain during the first seven years to feed the people and their animals during the seven years of famine.

Night Visions

At times, it may be challenging for the average person to know if a dream is of natural or spiritual origin. Some things to look for are:

- Natural dreams have no particular order and rapidly jump from scene to scene, person to person and circumstance to circumstance.
- Spiritual visions are usually very vivid and have a natural order.
- Spiritual visions will most often contain some type of symbolism.
- Spiritual visions are usually vividly intense, easily remembered and intensely real.

For the believer who knows God's Word, vision symbolism can be found throughout the Bible. Symbolism can also be drawn from one's life experiences. God uses symbols many times that only the person receiving the night vision will understand. Generally, if you spend the time to analyze your night vision against God's Word and your life's experiences the meaning will become clear. The Prophet Habakkuk tells us one way to remember our night visions is to write them down clearly and simply so their meaning is conveyed properly.

> Habakkuk 2:1–3—I will climb up to my watchtower and stand at my guard post. There I will wait to see what the Lord says and how he will answer my complaint. Then the Lord said to me, "Write my answer plainly on tablets, so that a runner can carry the correct message to others. This vision is for a future time. It describes the end, and it will be fulfilled. If it seems slow in coming, wait patiently, for it will surely take place. It will not be delayed.

Spiritual dreams and visions are a gift from God. They are an important way that God imparts to us a word of wisdom or a word of knowledge. As a believer, if you take the time to remember your dreams, God will speak to you.

Christian Cults and False Prophets

Not all who claim to have God-given visions can be trusted. The Bible warns against those who use so-called spiritual revelations to turn people away from the one true God and lead them into false worship. We find these false prophets in many Christian cults today.

> 1 John 5:20—And we know that the Son of God has come, and he has given us understanding so that we can know the true God. And now we live in fellowship with the true God because we live in fellowship with his Son, Jesus Christ. He is the only true God, and he is eternal life.

> Laminations 2:14—Your prophets have said so many foolish things, false to the core. They did not save you from exile by pointing out your sins. Instead, they painted false pictures, filling you with false hope.

How easily those who do not seek to know and understand the true Word of God are led astray by those who preach counterfeit doctrine. Go to the Word of God, verify the truth of a triune God and the Good News Gospel of Jesus Christ. Believe the Word that came directly from God. Go to the Word yourself and ask Him for the interpretation. He will speak to your heart.

Galatians 1:8—Let God's curse fall on anyone, including us or even an angel from heaven, who preaches a different kind of Good News than the one we preached to you.

Jeremiah 14:14—Then the LORD said, "These prophets are telling lies in my name. I did not send them or tell them to speak. I did not give them any messages. They prophesy of visions and revelations they have never seen or heard. They speak foolishness made up in their own lying hearts.

2 Corinthians 11:12–16—But I will continue doing what I have always done. This will undercut those who are looking for an opportunity to boast that their work is just like ours. These people are false apostles. They are deceitful workers who disguise themselves as apostles of Christ. But I am not surprised! Even Satan disguises himself as an angel of light. So it is no wonder that his servants also disguise themselves as servants of righteousness. In the end they will get the punishment their wicked deeds deserve.

Visions can be misleading

The Bible has many warnings about following false visions. Always confirm that a vision does not twist or contradict God's Word.

Spending the day upset, going to bed hungry or thirsty, eating a bad meal or any highly emotional state can result in a corresponding dream. These dreams are common and have little meaning.

> Isaiah 29:8—A hungry person dreams of eating, but wakes up still hungry. A thirsty person dreams of drinking, but is still faint from thirst when morning comes. So it will be with your enemies, with those who attack Mount Zion."

> Ecclesiastes 5:3—Too much activity gives you restless dreams; too many words make you a fool.

We must ask by what biblical standard, principle, or criteria are we to use to determine if a prophetic vision was a revelation from God? In seeking the answer, we must first go to the Bible to determine if it is in agreement with God's Word. The only standard God has given to us that does not change and is totally reliable is the inspired Word of His prophets, apostles, and the life of His Son. If your beliefs are not in accordance with God's Word, you are following false counsel.

2 Timothy 3:16–17—All Scripture is inspired by God and is useful to teach us what is true and to make us realize what is wrong in our lives. It corrects us when we are wrong and teaches us to do what is right. God uses it to prepare and equip his people to do every good work.

Hebrews 4:12—For the Word of God is alive and powerful. It is sharper than the sharpest two-edged sword, cutting between soul and spirit, between joint and marrow. It exposes our innermost thoughts and desires.

Jesus' apostles were simply disciples who knew beyond question that Jesus was the Son of God. They had witnessed His miracles, spoke with Him and spent time in His presence. The Apostolic Age began when the resurrected Jesus gave—The Great Commission—"go out into the world and make new disciples."

Matthew 28:16–20—Then the eleven disciples left for Galilee, going to the mountain where Jesus had told them to go. When they saw him, they worshiped him—but some of them doubted! Jesus came and told his disciples, "I have been given all authority in heaven and on earth. Therefore, go and make disciples of all the nations, baptizing them in the name of the Father and the Son and the Holy Spirit. Teach these new disciples to obey all the commands I have given you. And be sure of this: I am with you always, even to the end of the age."

The Apostolic Age ended with the death of the last apostle, the Apostle John, who died around AD 100.

Beware of any religious sect that claims to have their own translation of the Bible, offers any book considered to be a sacred addition to the Bible or adds to, twists, changes, or corrupts God's Word in any way.

Testing Your Spiritual Visions

If we can believe that some visions are spiritual and come from God, then we need to determine the origin of the vision. Some things you may want to look for are:

- Does the vision adhere to God's Word?
- Does the vision add strength to my faith?
- Does the vision promote goodness and love in my life and others?
- Does the vision encourage and help others?
- Does the vision follow the life of Jesus Christ?
- Does the vision reveal the character and virtues of Jesus?

Genesis 40:8—And they replied, "We both had dreams last night, but no one can tell us what they mean." "Interpreting dreams is God's business," Joseph replied. "Go ahead and tell me your dreams."

If there is any doubt that God has chosen to use this medium to speak to the Church, we only need to read the book of Isaiah. Isaiah was an anointed prophet of God. His visions speak of the coming Messiah and His ministry. No other prophet clearly and graphically prophesied the incarnation, birth, life, ministry and return of Christ.

My Personal Experience with Dreams and Visions

When I was about seven years old, I had to go to the hospital for an operation. A few days before I was to go, I had an encounter with two apparitions. I was lying in bed and about to fall asleep when two apparitions appeared—one on each side of my bed. They were a misty white, but very recognizable human forms. There was a man standing on the right side of my bed and a woman on the left, both were dressed in the nineteenth or early twentieth-century attire. He had on a top hat and suit; she was wearing a hat and a full dress. The woman sat down on my bed and put her hand on the area where I was to have my operation. I was so afraid that I did not move. When they finally disappeared, I was greatly relieved. That vision was burned into my memory and is just as vivid today as it was then. As a side note, the operation was a success. I have often wondered who they were. Given their interest in my area of discomfort I have come to believe they were doctors from an earlier time.

I began receiving spiritual visions several years ago when I started spending more and more time quietly meditating on God's Word and the world in which He lives. I refer to them as my personal visions from God because I believe these visions are for my spiritual edification, not for the Church.

My visions come as 3D colored or black and white pictures, living colored pictures that are vistas of beautiful landscapes, 3D cinemas that are similar to watching a live-action movie, and very symbolic live action short cinemas that require interpretation. Most of these visions occur during the night as I am falling asleep, or when I am just about to wake up. Although these visions only last for short periods of time they are indelibly recorded in my waking consciousness and always leave me with a profound since of joy and peace that lasts for days. I generally record them in my visions journal so I can review and enjoy them at a later time. I also have, on occasion, very real long lasting spiritual dreams of heavenly places.

Deathbed Visions

The stories of unexplained appearances by spirit beings that appear to dying patients have been well documented throughout recorded history. Those having these visions are seeing through the veil into the spiritual world. They speak of having been visited by Jesus, angels or by loved ones who had passed on. Sometimes they see beautiful vistas in the spiritual world and hear beautiful music.

There are also stories of horrifying visions of demons where these ugly ghoulish creatures were waiting for them to die. They sometimes speak of seeing a place of torment, despair and terrifying creatures.

These deathbed visions could be dismissed as hallucinations from a dying mind, except there are many times when doctors, nurses, family members, and others nearby have witnessed these visions along with the patient.

Deathbed visions were rarely seen in scientific literature until the late 1920's. Sir William Barrett, a professor of physics at the Royal College of Science in England became interested in deathbed visions when his wife, a doctor, told him about a woman who had died at the hospital that day after childbirth. Before she died the woman sat up and became very excited about seeing a wonderful place and said that her father and sister had come to take her there. The women was confused as to why her sister was there because her sister was still alive as far as she knew. The family had not told her about her sister's death three weeks earlier because of the way it may have affected her.

Professor Barrett found this story so interesting that he began a scientific study of deathbed visions. His was the first scientific study to find that even though some patients were so confused that they would just mumble or were not able to speak at all, the mind of the patient often became clear and rational before death. He also reported a number of cases in which the doctors, nurses and relatives present could also see what the dying patient saw. He published a book in 1926 called Deathbed Visions.

There are many cases on record with the Society of Psychical Research where the deathbed visions were seen by others at the bedside of the patient.

Visiting Heaven

I have always envisioned heaven as a beautiful and awesome place where we will worship our Creator in all we do and say. When we are not directly serving God, we will be able to travel to any of a countless number of vistas where we can enjoy the majesty of His eternal kingdom.

When I started researching the Bible, along with ancient Christian and Jewish literature for a presentable description of the afterlife realms of heaven and hell, I ran into a problem. I was unable to find a presentable description of what life in heaven or hell would be like.

What I did find were many ancient and modern descriptions of an afterlife based on personal accounts of journeys into the spiritual realms. Because the evidence derived from these accounts is purely empirical (proved or disproved by observation) I felt the need to do my own research. My research led me to the study of conscious dreaming, near-death experiences (NDE's), deathbed visions, out-of-body experiences (OBE's) and the accounts of those who were raised from the dead.

I decided to rely upon personal interviews and the documented evidence of those who were totally convinced of life beyond death. Although many of the experiences I studied were non-biblical, they were not anti-biblical.

Conscious Dreaming

I found Conscious Dreaming fascinating. It is when you become consciously aware that you are dreaming, and then you become either an objective dream observer or an active subjective participant in the dream.

For most of my life I had no idea that it was possible to become fully conscious in a dream. When I first started keeping a dream journal my paradoxical dreams were chaotic. Dream experiences did not follow any logical progression and would on occasion drift from scene to scene; a car would morph into a bicycle, a celebrity would change into a past acquaintance, a house would become an industrial center or the dream would just change completely in midstream. All this seemed quite normal while in the dream.

After about a week of studying conscious dreaming, I had my first fully conscious dream. I was so excited about watching my dream that I woke up as soon as it started. I later learned to sustain my conscious dreams for fifteen minutes or more.

A spiritual journey into the world where God lives

Although my conscious dreams have usually been more vivid than normal dreams, the dreams at times lacked the realism of life. But, occasionally I would have a dream that seemed dramatically more real than waking life. While in the dream, it felt like I woke from my dream and knew that I had somehow become fully conscious in another reality. I knew it was not a dream because I was fully conscious and completely aware of my faculties, knew who I was and where I was. I was also aware that my body was back in bed asleep. I could control my own actions and where I went in these new worlds, but like real life I generally had no control over other people or the environment I was in. I later realized that this type of experience was not considered a normal dream experience, but is known as a fully conscious spiritual dream. I have had many conscious dreams since I started recording them in 2010.

As I recorded and analyzed my conscious dreams, I began to be curious about who created them. Did I? If not who or what did? Where did the people, green grass, blue sky, mountains, waterfalls, trees, flowers, music, clouds, architecture, and other beautiful vistas come from? I am not particularly artistic, and I do not know of anyone who could create such aesthetically beautiful living places. As this spiritual questioning was going on, I realized that my senses did not provide any distinction between physical reality and spiritual reality while in the dream. I could feel, taste, smell, hear and see the same in the spiritual world as in the physical world. I could even talk and go places with people I met in these other worlds.

The experiences have been exciting, exhilarating and beyond anything I could have ever imagined. There is the realization of freedom where physical laws do not apply. You are able to transport yourself to other places in the wink of an eye, and if you want to take your time you can fly there. Sorry, no wings.

There are places of brilliant color, and extreme beauty that have no parallel in this world and everything in these other worlds displays God's grandeur. You can be transported to places where the feeling of God's love is a part of you. While there you realize His love is not just a feeling, but it emanates from everything around you.

There is no sun in the places I have visited, but there is light everywhere. I have talked and interacted with people who live in these places. I have flown over mountains, lakes, forests, and meadows where the beauty is incomparable to anything in this world. I have been in places so beautiful, serene and tranquil I wanted to stay there forever. I cannot tell you if I have truly visited heaven, but these otherworldly excursions have opened vistas so beautiful and full of love that it felt like heaven.

It was then I began to wonder; is it possible my visions were coming from the spiritual world? I am not able to be absolutely sure, but I lean heavily on the "Yes!" side. When I compared my visions against God's Word, I found no reason to believe they were not real heavenly excursions.

When I took another look at the biblical descriptions of heavenly visions, many of them sounded remarkably like my own conscious dreams. What I am sure of, is that there is an indescribable afterlife and it is on a much higher and grander scale than the world we live in.

Although conscious dreams of the heavenly realms are not common, they are very meaningful to those who have them. I have found that those who are spiritual, have a better chance of having a conscious dream because of their close relationship with Christ.

It is my hope that our Christian churches will wake up and open their minds to this phenomenon going on around them.

Habakkuk 2:2–3
Then the LORD said to me, "Write my answer plainly on tablets, so that a runner can carry the correct message to others. This vision is for a future time. It describes the end, and it will be fulfilled. If it seems slow in coming, wait patiently, for it will surely take place. It will not be delayed

Chapter Eleven

Caught up to Heaven

Revelations 4:1–3
Then as I looked, I saw a door standing open in heaven, and the same voice I had heard before spoke to me like a trumpet blast. The voice said, "Come up here, and I will show you what must happen after this." And instantly I was in the Spirit, and I saw a throne in heaven and someone sitting on it. The one sitting on the throne was as brilliant as gemstones—like jasper and carnelian. And the glow of an emerald circled his throne like a rainbow.

Heaven of Heavens

Scripture speaks of realms that are beyond the visible world. They are called the heavens of heaven. Since God is eternal, He is not restricted by geographical or spatial dimensions. God lives throughout the spiritual realms outside of space and time.

> 1 Kings 8:27—But will God really live on earth? Why, even the highest heavens cannot contain you. How much less this Temple I have built!

The heaven of heavens is not a place trillions of miles away, out there somewhere. Jesus tells us that the Kingdom of God is within us, and all around us. The Kingdom of God consists of many realms (dwelling places) which occupies the same physical space in which we live.

> Luke 17:20–21—One day the Pharisees asked Jesus, "When will the Kingdom of God come?" Jesus replied, "The Kingdom of God can't be detected by visible signs. You won't be able to say, 'Here it is!' or 'It's over there!' For the Kingdom of God is already among you (within you and around you)."

Heaven and Near-Death Experiences (NDEs)

The term "Near-Death Experience" was coined by Dr. Raymond Moody in his book "Life After Life." This term is used today to describe the stories of those who have died and returned to tell about their experiences. A medical NDE is when bodily functions completely cease or a brain scan using an EEG, Electroencephalograph, shows no brain activity and then the person comes back to life with a story to tell.

It is very important to remember that near-death experiences are subjective personal encounters, and although the empirical evidence for them is overwhelming, we will only know what heaven is truly like when we get there.

Throughout history, many thousands of people around the world tell of strikingly similar experiences while they were presumed to be dead and then came back to life. Many encounter a being that radiates a light of pure love and acceptance. While they are with this being, they experience a sense of peace and inexpressible joy. I have read a number of near-death experiences that describe this being as Jesus.

While most people want to remain with this being forever, they are sent back to their earthly life because they were told "it is not your time." Although the experience varies somewhat from person to person, it is consistently recounted as exciting and profoundly real.

As medical techniques advance, many people are being brought back to life from clinical death. Many of them talk about floating near the ceiling and seeing everything that happens around their bodies and then being transported through a tunnel to an alternate reality where they describe places beyond human imagination.

There are many books and Internet articles about those who have died, returned to life and believe to have experienced heaven. Many who have died and came back to life say they have seen their lost loved ones, their family, their friends, and even their pets. This is difficult to prove, yet the sheer number of those who have seen heaven and returned from death to tell about it is hard to refute.

There are many reasons why people believe NDEs are evidence of an afterlife and not simply the product of a dying brain.

- People see and hear things that would be impossible while they are unconscious.

    Patients who have been revived were able to describe in great technical detail exactly what was going on around then during the time they were supposedly unconscious or dead.

- Coming back with unexplained information.

    People having Near Death Experiences have returned with factual information of which they had no prior knowledge.

- Seeing the future.

    People came back with advanced knowledge of future events.

- People report being cured of a terminal illness.

- The blind can see during an NDE.

People who are blind, some of them from birth, were able to see during their near death experience.

- The aftereffects of an NDE are unique and long lasting.

People say that God is a part of everything they experience. There appear to be no atheists or humanists in heaven.

Skeptics would say that a near death experience was the result of the activity of a dying brain or a recovering brain; that no one can have an NDE while dead. NDEs of long brain-dead patients and the stories of those raised from the dead completely disproved this idea.

What is a Near-Death Experience Like?

Most Christians have spent at least some time in their life wondering what heaven will be like. Those who have had a heavenly NDE say they know absolutely what heaven is like, and they no longer fear death.

Many of us today are familiar with the testimonies of people who have had near-death experiences. But each of these accounts is unique, and can only give us a glimpse of what heaven may be like.

This phenomenon has played a major role and become a major influence as to how many people now see life after death. There is a consensus among those who have had an NDE that heaven consists of many dwelling places, (realms, dimensions, or planes of existence). NDEs help us to understand and affirm that there are a number of majestic dwelling places we could enter after death. These dwelling places are said to be segmented and organized around qualities of love, service, and personal preparedness. The reports of the many individuals who have been permitted to see or visit these dwelling places tell us they are located around our physical world.

Those who have had an NDE tell us that after physical death we will be acutely aware of everything we have rightly done or failed to do in our lives. When we enter our place in the spiritual world, we will be able to know the thoughts of those around us and they will know ours. Therefore, we will be with those who think the same as we do and those whose values are the same as ours. Each realm is said to correspond to a particular level of spiritual development—or lack of it.

The exception to this is that those who have been redeemed by the sacrificial blood of Jesus go directly to the heaven of heavens—Paradise.

Heavenly Dwelling Places

Near-death experiencers tell us that when we die our entire life is reviewed and then those who do not know Christ travel a specific path in the spiritual world. Some paths lead to heavenly dwelling places and some paths lead to hellish dwelling places. There are people who believe the things of this world have no consequence. Nothing is farther from the truth.

> Matthew 16:27—For the Son of Man will come with his angels in the glory of his Father and will judge all people according to their deeds.

> Revelations 22:12—Look, I am coming soon, bringing my reward with me to repay all people according to their deeds.

Those who have accepted the salvation offered by our Lord and Savior Jesus Christ, will travel to the heaven of heavens—Paridise.

Our love for God and our neighbors, or lack of it, is said to make up a realm of destiny within us; the realm we will inherit upon death. This realm is made known to us after death when our thoughts and feelings reach out to a particular heavenly or hellish community. Heavenly communities are reached if our strongest love matches the love of a particular heavenly realm. Hellish communities are reached if our lack of love matches a particular hellish realm. All hellish realms are said to be dark, cold and inhospitable. Those that have been there and returned to tell about it, say the sad lives of the spirits there matched their own.

The central factor determining your particular place is the degree to which you showed love to all of God's Creation and helped others along their spiritual journey.

In this respect, your acts of loving kindness carry the greatest rewards.

It is believed by some that the heavenly dwelling places surrounding us are a matter of progressively lighter (or higher) spiritual vibrations and the hellish dwelling places are a matter of progressively lower (or denser) spiritual vibrations. And that our world is right in between. The dwelling place of those who have not accepted the salvation offered by Jesus are entered after death based on the amount of spiritual energy they attained on earth. The greater the love the finer the vibration and the higher they will ascend into the heavenly realms.

Heavier vibrations represent the negative nature in the darkness of this world and the heavier the vibration, the farther they descend into the hellish realms. People do not enter the light or dark realms because of their good deeds or bad deeds, but because their soul vibration takes them there. They say our soul naturally fits in the place we have created within us in this world. These places vary from extreme suffering and torment to places of happiness and joy. This means we are not going to heaven, so much as it comes to us. Many who have had an oppressive NDE have changed their lives to become better stewards of their earthly home and devout followers of Jesus Christ.

When we are redeemed through the blood of our Lord and Savior, Jesus Christ, our soul vibrates at a divine level and we will enter the Heaven of heavens (Paradise) where Jesus reigns.

Hellish Dwelling Places

There are hundreds of stories from all over the world of those who have visited hell. After reading many of these stories, I was surprised by how remarkably similar they were.

All hellish NDEs have a common theme of seeing hellish images and being tortured by vile creatures not of this world. I chose the following two NDE stories of hell because of their common depiction of the places in hell. The places in hell described in these stories are representative of the many hellish dwelling places I have studied.

Saint Faustina's visit to hell in 1936

Saint Faustina was a nun who lived in Poland. She was canonized by Pope John Paul 2 on April 30, 2000. She speaks of seven dwelling places in hell and believes hell is eternal.

> "Our Lord had her to visit Hell in 1936. Here is her awesome account of this horrifying and dreadful place: "Today, I was led by an Angel to the chasms of hell. It is a place of great torture; how awesomely large and extensive it is! The kinds of tortures I saw: the first torture that constitutes hell is the loss of God; the second is perpetual remorse of conscience; the third is that one's condition will never change; the fourth is the fire that will penetrate the soul without destroying it—a terrible suffering, since it

is a purely spiritual fire, lit by God's anger; the fifth torture is continual darkness and a terrible suffocating smell, and, despite the darkness, the devils and the souls of the damned see each other and all the evil, both of others and their own; the sixth torture is the constant company of Satan; the seventh torture is the horrible despair, hatred of God, vile words, curses, and blasphemies.

These are the tortures suffered by all the damned together, but that is not the end of the sufferings. There are special tortures destined for particular souls.

These are the torments of the senses. Each soul undergoes terrible and indescribable sufferings, related to the manner in which it has sinned. There are caverns and pits of torture where one form of agony differs from another. I would have died at the very sight of these tortures if the omnipotence of God had not supported me. Let the sinner know that he will be tortured throughout all eternity, in those senses which he made use of to sin. I am writing this at the command of God, so that no soul may find an excuse by saying there is no hell, or that nobody has ever been there, and so no one can say what it is like. I, Sister Faustina, by the order of God, have visited the abysses of hell so that I might tell souls about it and testify to its existence. I cannot speak about it now; but I have received a command from God to leave it in writing. The devils were full of hatred for me, but they had to obey me at the command of God. What I have written is but a pale shadow of the things I saw. But I noticed one thing: that most of the souls there are those who disbelieved that there is a hell. When I came to, I could hardly recover from the fright. How terribly souls suffer there! Consequently, I pray even more fervently for the conversion of sinners. I incessantly plead God's mercy upon them. O my Jesus, I would rather be in agony until the end of the world, amidst the greatest sufferings, than offend You by the least sin."

Retrieved 10/4/2013 from <http://www.bibleprobe.com/hell-is-real.htm>.

Pastor Howard Storm's book "My Descent Into Death"

The following is a summary of Pastor Howard Stone's near-death experience from his book "My Descent Into Death." I chose this particular story of hell because it contains the best representation and commonality of all the hell narratives I have read. This summary was written by Kevin Williams. Because of its length I have left out parts of Pastor Storm's narrative while hopefully still retaining its profound insights. I had the unique experience of briefly speaking with Pastor Stone. I talked with him about his book and asked for his permission to reprint Kevin William's article. He gave me permission to reprint any part of his book. At the time of Howard Stone's NDE he was not a pastor. This NDE summary, in its entirety can be found on Kevin Williams web site at www.near-death.com/storm.

Before his near-death experience, Howard Storm was a Professor of Art at Northern Kentucky University and was not a very pleasant man by his own admission. He was an avowed atheist and was hostile to every form of religion and those who practiced it. He knew with certainty that the material world was the full extent of everything that was. He considered all belief systems associated with religion to be fantasies for people to deceive themselves with. Beyond what science said, there was nothing else. But then on June 1, 1985, at the age of 38, Howard Storm had a near-death experience due to a perforation of the stomach and his life was forever changed. His near-death experience is one of the most profound afterlife-experience I have ever documented. His life was so immensely changed after his near-death experience that he resigned as a professor and devoted his time attending the United Theological Seminary to become a United Church of Christ minister. Today, Howard Storm is presently happily married to his wife Marcia and is Pastor of the Covington United Church of Christ in Covington, Ohio.

The following is the account of Pastor Howard Storm's near-death experience reprinted with permission.

-An Invitation to Hell from Strange Beings-

Struggling t0o look back and see the hospital room. My body was still there lying motionless on the bed.

Walking for what seemed to be a considerable distance, these beings were all around me. They were leading me through the haze. I don't know how long. As we traveled, the fog got thicker and darker, and the people began to change. At first they seemed rather playful and happy, but when we had covered some distance, a few of them began to get aggressive.

A wild orgy of frenzied taunting, screaming and hitting ensued. I fought like a wild man. All the while it was obvious that they were having great fun. It seemed to be, almost, a game for them, with me as the center-piece of their amusement. My pain became their pleasure. They seemed to want to make me hurt by clawing at me and biting me. Whenever I would get one off me, there were five more to replace the one.

My attempts to fight back only provoked greater merriment. They began to physically humiliate me in the most degrading ways. They were playing with me just as a cat plays with a mouse. Every new assault brought howls of cacophony. Then at some point, they began to tear off pieces of my flesh. To my horror I realized I was being taken apart and eaten alive, slowly, so that their entertainment would last as long a possible.

Fighting well and hard for a long time, ultimately I was spent. Lying there exhausted amongst them, they began to calm down since I was no longer the amusement that I had been. By this time I had been pretty much taken apart. People were still picking at me, occasionally, and I just lay there all torn up, unable to resist.

Exactly what happened was . . . and I'm not going to try and explain this. From inside of me I felt a voice, my voice, say, "Pray to God." I started saying things like, "The Lord is my shepherd, I shall not want . . . God bless America" and anything else that seemed to have a religious connotation. And these people went into a frenzy, as if I had thrown boiling oil all over them.

They began yelling and screaming at me, telling me to quit, that there was no God, and no one could hear me. While they screamed and yelled obscenities, they also began backing away from me as if I were poison. As they were retreating, they became more rabid, cursing and screaming that what I was saying was worthless and that I was a coward. I screamed back at them, "Our Father who art in heaven," and similar ideas. This continued for some time until, suddenly, I was aware that they had left. It was dark, and I was alone yelling things that sounded churchy. It was pleasing to me that these churchy sayings had such an effect on those awful beings.

-A Rescue from Hell by Jesus Christ-

The agony that I had suffered during the day was nothing compared to what I was feeling now. I knew then that this was the absolute end of my existence, and it was more horrible than anything I could possibly have imagined.

Then a most unusual thing happened. I heard very clearly, once again in my own voice, something that I had learned in nursery Sunday School. It was the little song, "Jesus loves me, yes I know . . ." and it kept repeating. I don't know why, but all of a sudden I wanted to believe that. Not having anything left, I wanted to cling to that thought. And I, inside, screamed, "Jesus, please save me." That thought was screamed with every ounce of strength and feeling left in me. When I did that, I saw, off in the darkness somewhere, the tiniest little star. Not knowing what it was, I presumed it must be a comet or a meteor, because it was moving rapidly.

Then I realized it was coming toward me. It was getting very bright, rapidly. When the light came near, its radiance spilled over me, and I just rose up—not with my effort—I just lifted up. Then I saw—and I saw this very plainly—I saw all my wounds, all my tears, all my brokenness, melt away. And I became whole in this radiance. What I did was to cry uncontrollably. I was crying, not out of sadness, but because I was feeling things that I had never felt before in my life.

The light conveyed to me that it loved me in a way that I can't begin to express. It loved me in a way that I had never known that love could possibly be. He was a concentrated field of energy, radiant in splendor indescribable, except to say goodness and love. I could feel its light on me—like very gentle hands around me. And I could feel it holding me. But it was loving me with overwhelming power. After what I had been through, to be completely known, accepted, and intensely loved by this Being of Light surpassed anything I had known or could have imagined.

We started going faster and faster, out of the darkness. Embraced by the light, feeling wonderful and crying, I saw off in the distance something that looked like the picture of a galaxy, except that it was larger and there were more stars than I had seen on Earth. There was a great center of brilliance. In the center there was an enormously bright concentration. Outside the center countless millions of spheres of light were flying about entering and leaving what was a great being-ness at the center. It was off in the distance.

For the first time he spoke to my mind in a male voice and told me that if I was uncomfortable we didn't have to go closer. So we stopped where we were, still countless miles away from the Great being. For the first time, my friend, and I will refer to him in that context hereafter, said to me, "You belong here." Facing all the splendor made me acutely aware of my lowly condition. My response was: "No, you've made a mistake, put me back." And he said, "We don't make mistakes. You belong."

Then he called out in a musical tone to the luminous entities who surrounded the great center. Several came and circled around us. These beings were giving me what I needed at that time. To my surprise, and also distress, they seemed to be capable of knowing everything I was thinking. I didn't know whether I would be capable of controlling my thoughts and keeping anything secret. We began to engage in thought exchange, conversation that was very natural, very easy and casual. I heard their voices clearly and individually. They each had a distinct personality with a voice, but they spoke directly to my mind, not my ears. And they used normal, colloquial English.

-The Life Review of Howard Storm-

To my surprise my life played out before me, maybe six or eight feet in front of me, from beginning to end. The life review was very much in their control, and they showed me my life, but not from my point of view. I saw me in my life and this whole thing was a lesson, even though I didn't know it at the time. They were trying to teach me something, but I didn't know it was a teaching experience, because I didn't know that I would be coming back. We just watched my life from beginning to the end. Some things they slowed down on, and zoomed in on and other things they went right through.

My life was shown in a way that I had never thought of before. All of the things that I had worked to achieve, the recognition that I had worked for, in elementary school, in high school, in college, and in my career, they meant nothing in this setting.

What they responded to was how I had interacted with other people. That was the long and short of it. Unfortunately, most of my interactions with other people didn't measure up with how I should have interacted, which was in a loving way. Whenever I did react during my life in a loving way.

They rejoiced. Every time I got a little upset they turned the life's review off for awhile, and they just loved me. Their love was tangible. You could feel it on your body, you could feel it inside you; their love went right through you. I wish I could explain it to you, but I can't.

When the review was finished they asked, "Do you want to ask any questions?" and I had a million questions. I asked, for example, "What about the Bible?" They responded, "What about it?" I asked if it was true, and they said it was.

They told me that it contained spiritual truth, and that I had to read it spiritually in order to understand it. It should be read prayerfully. My friends informed me that it was not like other books. They also told me, and I later found out this was true, that when you read it prayerfully, it talks to you. It reveals itself to you. And you don't have to work at it anymore.

Asking them if there was life on other planets, their surprising answer was that the universe was full of life.

-Howard Storm Learns What Happens After Death-

I asked my friend, and his friends, about death—what happens when we die?

They said that when a loving person dies, angels come down to meet him, and they take him up—gradually, at first, because it would be unbearable for that person to be instantly exposed to God.

Knowing what's inside of every person, the angels don't have to prove anything by showing off. They know what each of us needs, so they provide that. We see what is necessary for our introduction into the spirit world, and those things are real, in the heavenly, the divine sense.

They gradually educate us as spirit beings, and bring us into heaven. We grow and increase, and grow and increase, and shed the concerns, desires, and base animal stuff that we have been fighting much of our life. Earthly appetites melt away. It is no longer a struggle to fight them. We become who we truly are, which is part of the divine.

This happens to loving people, people who are good and love God. They made it clear to me that we don't have any knowledge or right to judge anybody else—in terms of that person's heart relationship to

God. Only God knows what's in a person's heart. Someone whom we think is despicable, God might know as a wonderful person. Similarly, someone we think is good, God may see as a hypocrite, with a black heart. Only God knows the truth about every individual.

God will ultimately judge every individual. And God will allow people to be dragged into darkness with like-minded creatures. I have told you, from my personal experience, what goes on in there. I don't know from what I saw anymore than that, but it's my suspicion that I only saw the tip of the iceberg.

Life in the Heavenly Dwelling Places

Like the teachings of Jesus, heavenly near-death experiences reveal the critical importance of divine love in all facets of life and death. These near-death experiences complement Jesus' teachings of unconditional love and forgiveness. In fact, an experience of God's unconditional love is the most prominent feature of heavenly NDE's.

> Luke 10:25–28—One day an expert in religious law stood up to test Jesus by asking him this question: "Teacher, what should I do to inherit eternal life?" Jesus replied, "What does the law of Moses say? How do you read it?" The man answered, "'You must

love the Lord your God with all your heart, all your soul, all your strength, and all your mind.' And, 'Love your neighbor as yourself.'" "Right!" Jesus told him. "Do this and you will live!"

People who have had a heavenly near-death experience have a lot to say about the spiritual dwelling places concerning the relationship between life on Earth and life there. In every case our lives on earth pales in every way to life in the heavenly realms.

Those who have had an NDE say that their events in the heavenly realms are real, not a dream or hallucination. They claim to have had an experience of a life with feelings so pure and deep that they are far beyond anything in this world. The Apostle Paul tells us that heaven, from a human standpoint is indescribable.

> 1 Corinthians 2:9—That is what the Scriptures mean when they say: "No eye has seen, no ear has heard, and no mind has imagined what God has prepared for those who love him."

NDE experiencers tell us that in heaven, there are no inhibitions or need for them. Everyone does exactly as their will dictates. This works out very well because only the best in each person survives and good is all anyone wants to do. There is a freedom and happiness in heaven that people on earth cannot imagine.

Our current senses of hearing, seeing, smelling, tasting, and touching are only poor reflections of the greater senses we will experience in the afterlife. The spiritual body can travel by thought. If one thinks of a person or location, one can immediately be transported there. Communication is by thought. In the spiritual world, we are completely free from the restrictions of a physical shell. We have the opportunity to continue our progress as a soul, to choose our vocation, and to experience complete and unconditional love.

What we do in the heavenly realms depends on our interests and desires. The skills, interests, and abilities developed on earth may be reflected in the roles chosen in eternity. Each of us will serve God and contribute uniquely toward the goodness and beauty in the place we live.

People who were married on earth may meet in heaven and recognize one another. Although they are no longer married, because of their love for each other they may stay together. We will be able to spend time with our family and friends who are there with us.

The heavenly places are always characterized by abounding love, vivid greenness, crystalline cleanliness, newness, and overall beauty, all of which are maintained by God and His angels. Everything in heaven is pure and always bright and new.

Going Home

Near-death accounts provide a general progression of what transpires after we die. These NDE accounts have helped to build the faith of those who encountered them and those who have read about them. The following are themes that run through many NDE experiences.

- Just before death comes, various unusual visual or auditory sensations occur.
- Extremely pleasant feelings and sensations occur during the early stages after death.
- People find themselves out of their body and can observe what is happening around them.
- People feel as if heaven has always been their home.
- After a short while they enter something that resembles a tunnel.
- When they enter the tunnel a brilliant light can be seen at the far end.
- Once they traverse the tunnel and enter the light they find themselves in incredibly brilliant white light, where they are overwhelmed with love, peace, joy, and incredible beauty.
- Knowledge beyond our deepest dreams exists there.
- Everyone enters a receiving station where their life review occurs. The life review shows them their spiritual strengths and shortcomings so they will understand why they must enter a particular place. But no matter which dwelling place they

qualify for, each dwelling place is so superior to any place on earth it is virtually indescribable.
- Throughout all of the heavenly places there is no condemnation for past transgressions; only compassion and love.
- Even though family and friends may live in different places, they are reunited and can spend time with one another throughout eternity.
- Heavenly vistas can be experienced such as exquisite valleys and meadows, beautiful gardens, crystal lakes, rippling rivers, majestic mountains, sparkling waterfalls, and dwellings of impressive architecture. There are vistas of endless possibilities for creativity and the full realization of your dreams and desires.
- Further spiritual growth can be realized, and it may be decided to enter spiritual training.
- The right to inhabit a higher dwelling place, if so desired may be earned.
- Many who have had an NDE claim to have had supernatural abilities such as:

  - 360-degree vision
  - Being in two different locations at the same time
  - Travel instantaneously
  - Read the minds of others
  - Being outside of space and time
  - Hearing heavenly music
  - Creating things with their mind
  - Talking with Angels

- Once in heaven, a person knows this is their true home.

Jeremiah 1:5—I knew you before I formed you in your mother's womb. Before you were born I set you apart and appointed you as my prophet to the nations."

Psalms 139:15–16—You watched me as I was being formed in utter seclusion, as I was woven together in the dark of the womb. You saw me before I was born. Every day of my life was recorded in your book. Every moment was laid out before a single day had passed.

Heavenly Structures

Many who believe in God and have had an NDE, have described seeing many places mentioned in the Bible: God's throne, His temple, New Jerusalem, the city of God, and a crystal city of light and gold.

Some other descriptions include golden cities of light with towers and domes, cities of crystal cathedrals, beautiful fairy tale like cities, cities that represent entire worlds, multi-colored crystal cities, endless and brilliant cities with beautiful music and colorful light, galaxy-like cities of lights, a heavenly city in the clouds where spirits leave to come to earth and where spirits go to after death. In these cities are libraries of wisdom, halls of spiritual learning, temples of worship, and family communities.

Around the cities are waterfalls, mountains, valleys, forests, meadows, and lakes there for our enjoyment.

Visiting Heaven

Heaven is truly a spiritual state of living with love, peace, and joy. In heaven, we are where we were meant to be before the fall of Adam. In heaven there is a perfect freedom of spirit and no one ever abuses this freedom or feels unwanted or unloved.

God's presence is so real that we are never alone or without spiritual guidance. The love of God in heaven is like the air we breathe here on earth. The beauty of heaven is beyond imagination and reflects back upon those who dwell there the intense serenity of belonging.

Pastor Don Piper's Near-Death Experience.

One very famous case of an NDE is about a Baptist minister, Don Piper, who appeared to have died when a 16-wheeler smashed into his Ford Escort head-on while he was crossing a bridge. Amazingly, he is still around to tell about his heavenly excursion. He recounted the story of his heavenly journey in his book "90 Minutes in Heaven."

> I was killed instantly. I was immediately struck, crushed by the roof of the car collapsing, steering wheel impaling me on the chest, and the dashboard collapsing on both of my legs. Paramedics could

find no sign of life at all in Piper, and placed a tarp over him while waiting for the medical examiner to arrive. A fellow priest prayed over him, but as he was singing "What a Friend We Have in Jesus," Piper began singing along. This was an hour and a half after he was assumed dead. Where did Piper go? To hear him tell it, he died and went to heaven. Piper wrote a best-selling book, "90 Minutes in Heaven," in which he details being at the Pearly Gates, seeing other believers, hearing songs never heard on earth and thinking only good thoughts. He has now established a ministry based upon his death experience.

I highly recommend Pastor Piper's book "90 Minutes in Heaven" because it is probably one of the most dramatic descriptions of the spiritual reality found within an NDE narrative. It demonstrates how the power of faith is transformed into absolute certainty about God and His waiting Kingdom.

Dr. George Ritchie's Near-Death Experience.

The following is a narrative of Dr. Richie's near-death experience, and his life review from his book "Return from Tomorrow." The narrative was written by Kevin Williams and was retrieved from his web site website— www.near-death.com.

George Ritchie dies of pneumonia in a Texas Army hospital and leaves his body unaware that he is dead.

Caught up to Heaven

He wanders around the hospital ward and wonders why people cannot see or hear him. Wanting eagerly to travel to Richmond, Virginia, to finish college, the thought instantly sends him flying through the door of the hospital and into the air—traveling thousands of miles toward Richmond. He is bewildered about these sudden supernatural powers of flight and transparency he has attained. He then arrives at a city with a bar and discovers the people there cannot see or hear him either. He also has no solidness there. He flies back to the Army hospital where he sees his lifeless body in the morgue and realizes he is dead.

Suddenly, a being of tremendous light and love appears before him. Ritchie realizes this light is like "a million welders' lamps all blazing at once." Human eyes would be destroyed in a second if they saw it. The being tells Ritchie to stand up. Ritchie is astonished to learn he is standing before Jesus Christ. More than anything emanating from Jesus was the unbelievable amount of unconditional love shining from him—a love that knew everything about Ritchie and loved him just the same. Simultaneously, as Jesus appeared to him, Ritchie watches his entire life displayed before him. Jesus asks him, "What have you done with your life?" Ritchie tries to come up with several examples but realizes he has fallen short. Ritchie eventually realizes Jesus is not judging him at all; but rather,

Ritchie was judging himself. And the question, "What have you done with your life?" had more to do with "How much unconditional love have you given others."

-Dr. Richie's Guided Tour of the Earthbound Realm with Jesus-

Then Jesus begins to take Ritchie on a journey through various realms of the afterlife. They fly toward a large city on Earth where they notice a group of assembly-line workers at work. They witness the spirit of a woman trying desperately to grab a cigarette from the workers who were oblivious to her presence. This woman had died severely addicted to cigarettes and was now cut off from the one thing she desperately desired most.

Ritchie realizes how the spirits in these realms immediately know the thoughts of other spirits around them. This is the reason they tend to group together with other spirits. It is too threatening to be around others who knew and disagreed with their thoughts.

They then travel to a bar somewhere on Earth which is filled with sailors drinking heavily. Spirits surrounded the sailors as they try desperately, and in vain, to grasp the shot glasses to get a drink. Other spirits try to control the sailors' alcoholic behavior.

Ritchie learns these are the spirits of people who died still having a severe alcoholic addiction that went beyond the physical. He is bewildered as he observes one of the sailors passing out causing the sailor's protective aura surrounding him to crack open. When it does, it allows a spirit to scramble into the sailor's unconscious body. This scene was repeated over and over.

-Dr. Richie's description of the horrors of hell-

They were still somewhere on the surface of the Earth; but no living person or beings of light could be seen. Before them was a plain jammed with hordes of spirits who are the most miserable and angriest beings he has ever seen. Many were engaged in hand-to-hand combat with no weapons—trying in vain to hurt and kill those who did not agree with them. A lot of verbal abuse could be heard between them as their thoughts could be heard by everyone around them the moment they were thought. Ritchie is horrified as he wonders what living in such a realm would be like—a place where you cannot hide from who you really are. These spirits were locked into destructive thought-patterns, rage and uncontrollable lust. Some were trying in vain to get sexual gratification from each other. The wailing coming from the hordes of unsatisfied spirits was tremendous. Other spirits were in despair saying things such as, "I always knew!" and "Didn't I warn you!" Ritchie realizes this place is truly hell . Their obsessive thoughts and emotions extended beyond the physical realm and into the spiritual realm where they cannot be satisfied. Yet there was nothing preventing any of the poor spirits in these realms from leaving. There was no condemnation coming from Jesus either—only compassion for these miserable spirits. Ritchie realizes Jesus had not abandoned any of them here. Instead they fled from the light to escape from having the darkness of their hearts openly revealed.

-Dr. Richie's Vision of the Heavenly City-

Ritchie is then taken into outer space toward a distant city made of brilliant light—similar in description to the heavenly city in the Book of Revelation 21:10–27. This is the place where people go who have become like Jesus while on Earth—a place where love is the dominant focus of life. This is heaven he realizes; but he is not allowed to enter it. Instead, Jesus shows him the future of Earth and is told to return to his physical body. At this point, Ritchie is revived from death.

Colton Burpo's NDE, "Heaven is for Real"

The following is a brief summary of Colton Burpo's near-death experience from his Father's book, "Heaven is for real." I selected this NDE because it contains an innocent child's account of heaven.

> Colton Burpo, the three-year-old son of Todd and Sonja Burpo, spent time in heaven and returned to tell about it. Colton had a ruptured appendix that had been poisoning his body for several days. Close to death, he was taken into surgery. While it was a very close call, the surgery was a success. Colton's parents were continually in prayer during his operation.
>
> Over time, Colton explained to his parents what happened to him when he died and was taken to heaven. The book is filled with account after account of Colton telling his parents about his time with Jesus. Things Colton could not have known at such a young age were told to his bewildered parents.

The following summary from "Heaven is for Real" was used with permission from Thomas Nelson Publishing.

-The main events of Colton's experience-

- He sat in Jesus' lap.
- He met his sister who died in his mother's womb (whom his parents had never told him about).
- He saw John the Baptist.
- There is a coming battle with Satan.

- There are thousands of colors we have never seen.
- He met his great granddad who told him things about his father that his father had never told him.
- He saw Jesus' "marks" on his hands and feet.
- All the people had wings of various sizes (including Colton) and flew around (except Jesus, who moved up and down as if on an escalator).
- Jesus had the most beautiful eyes, a beard, a white gown, a purple sash, and a crown.
- All the people had a light above their head.
- Jesus sits on a throne at the right hand of God and Gabriel is on the left.
- He sat by God the Holy Spirit (who he could not describe) and explained to his dad that God is three people.
- It never gets dark in heaven because God the Father and God the Son are the lights.
- There were all kinds of animals everywhere.
- Nobody is old in heaven, and no one wears glasses.
- Jesus "shoots" power down from heaven to his father while he is preaching.
- The gates to heaven are made of gold and pearls.

Akiane Kramarik, Jesus is for real

The following is a brief summary of Akiane Kramarik's experience with God and her heavenly encounters. Although not a near-death experience, I selected Akiane's encounter with God because it also comes from a young child who, along with another young child, Colton Burpo, confirms the face of Jesus.

The following narrative from their book "Her Life, Her Art, Her Poetry" was used with permission from Thomas Nelson Publishing.

> Akiane Kramarik was born 1994 in Mount Morris, Illinois to a Lithuanian mother and an American father. Akiane and her siblings grew up in a nurturing home where the children were mainly homeschooled. During the early years of Akiane's life the family had few friends, no relatives, and no television or radio. They were atheists, so when Akiane began telling her mother at age three about her spiritual visions where God spoke to her they were taken by surprise. She said that God told her that she should paint and draw the visions He gave her. When her mother asked her how she knew that it was God speaking to her, she replied, "Because I can hear His voice, His voice is quiet and beautiful." But the words I speak to Him are different; I speak to Him through my mind." Although her family did not believe in God at the time they fully supported her.
>
> Akiane told her family that her encounters with God were real. At age four she began to have very vivid and colorful dreams and visions of other dimensions and a great desire to express them

A spiritual journey into the world where God lives

through art and poetry. She began by drawing her visions and by age six she was painting them. Akiane's passion for God, along with her artwork and poetry inspired her parents to reevaluate their atheistic lifestyle. Her mother said that because of Akiane their family went through a spiritual awakening and became Christians.

At nine years of age Akiane appeared on the Oprah Winfrey show. Her unique gifts came through as she shared them with the audience and the world. The media took note and her fame spread all over the world. Akiane's mother, Forelli Kramarik, and Akiane wrote a book called "Her Life, Her Art, Her Poetry."

One morning when Akiane was four, she began sharing her visions of heaven with us.

"Today I met God," Akiane whispered to me one morning.

"What is God?" I was surprised to hear this. To me, God's name always sounded absurd and primitive.
"God is light warm and good. It knows everything and talks with me. It is my parent."
"Tell me more about your dream"
"It was not a dream. It was real!" I looked at her slightly puffed eyes, and in complete disbelief
I kept on asking her questions.

"So who is your God?"
"Just like I know you are my mommy, and you know I am Akiane."
"Who even taught you such a word as God?"
"You won't understand."

It was not long before her parents realized that Akiane's encounters with God and other dimensions of reality were not coming from this world. Akiane was seeing into and experiencing the spiritual world. Akiane, on Facebook, talking about Jesus tells us about Jesus.

"Jesus remains my highest authority, love, and God."

"I pray every day that people will one day follow Jesus, His teachings and feel His love."

"He is the only way to God—the only way to heaven and joy."

"My personal views on Jesus have only matured and deepened since age 4. As I grow I see how vast and unlimited His love is." Jesus is Love. He is the only way to God, the only way to Heaven and Joy. ~Akiane

At the age of eight she was inspired to paint the face of Jesus, based on her encounters with Him. She named her painting "The Prince of Peace." Colton

Burpo, in the book "Heaven is for Real," identified this painting of Jesus as the closest representation of Jesus whom he had seen during his near-death experience.

Both Akiane and Colton talked about the beauty of Jesus' eyes. "All I remember were the eyes," Akiane says, "and they were like no other colors that were ever created. The closest color I can depict through paints is a sapphire hue." Colton identified the color of Jesus' eyes as blue-green.

To view Akiane's paintings visit her website at www.artakiane.com.

Corinthians 12:2–4

I was caught up to the third heaven fourteen years ago. Whether I was in my body or out of my body, I don't know—only God knows. Yes, only God knows whether I was in my body or outside my body. But I do know that I was caught up to paradise and heard things so astounding that they cannot be expressed in words, things no human is allowed to tell.

Closing Thoughts

God Wants You to be with Him in His Eternal Kingdom

We came to earth to fulfill a divine purpose, and each of us has a very different reason for being here. We did not come here just to consume resources and take up space; we came to grow in Spirit and to make a positive difference in the world around us. We also came to earth to make a contribution to the welfare of others and in all ways to glorify our Creator. We can open ourselves to the beautiful and the divine work of God or we can tread along life without the awesome and wonderful things God has to offer.

If you feel you have done too many bad things for God to forgive you, then you are wrong. There is no sin too great for God to forgive. His love for you covers any and all sins when you accept Him as Lord. If there was a sin too big or too horrible for God to forgive, then God could not be God.

When we try to hold on to the world without God, we soon realize the things of this world are temporary and we are left alone with a wanting in our hearts for an understanding of who we truly are and why we exist at all. There is no greater reward in this life than to know who we truly are and that we can live forever in God's eternal Kingdom.

Jesus is the key to His Father's Kingdom. To enter God's Eternal Kingdom you must lay your sins at the foot of the cross and accept Jesus' offer of forgiveness. Jesus has an open door policy. If you ask Him in, He will cross the threshold of your heart and take up residence. Then He is able to open doors to places you have only dreamed of. The road He will lead you on is narrow and at times quite difficult, but the rewards are greater than anything you could ever imagine. Ask Jesus to take up residence in your heart, follow Him daily, and watch for beautiful events to unfold in your life.

If the desire of your heart is to move from this life into God's Eternal Kingdom, pray this simple prayer with reverence and meaning.

> Heavenly Father, I confess with my mouth that Your Son Jesus freely laid down His life on the Cross of Calvary and shed His blood so that anyone who would accept Him as Lord would be saved. He was raised from the dead and now reigns in His Fathers eternal Kingdom. I lay my sins at the foot of the

Cross and accept You, Jesus, as my Lord and Savior. Amen!

Following in the footsteps of Jesus is a path of self-discipline, acts of willpower, patience, restraint, resolve, determination, self-control, courage, and persistence.

Every new Christian has the challenge of maintaining control over their thoughts, appetites, speech, temper, and desires. High ethical values and moral traits are to be deliberately developed and cultivated. When you walk in Jesus' footsteps, you will walk with Him right into eternity.

To have the Heart and Mind of Jesus is to have an Eternal Mindset

I hope at least something in this book has touched your heart and brought you closer to God. Your call to heaven is toll-free, and God is waiting on an open line!

I leave you with an inspirational prayer written by the Apostle Paul to the church in Ephesus.

Ephesians 3:16–21

I pray that from his glorious, unlimited resources he will empower you with inner strength through his Spirit. Then Christ will make his home in your hearts as you trust in him. Your roots will grow down into God's love and keep you strong. And may you have the power to understand, as all God's people should, how wide, how long, how high, and how deep his love is. May you experience the love of Christ, though it is too great to understand fully. Then you will be made complete with all the fullness of life and power that comes from God. Now all glory to God, who is able, through his mighty power at work within us, to accomplish infinitely more than we might ask or think. Glory to him in the church and in Christ Jesus through all generations forever and ever! Amen.

Bibliography

The following works were consulted during the writing of this book and are invaluable resources for anyone interested in learning about the awesome spiritual side of life.

A. Leo Oppenheim, "Mantic Dreams in the Ancient Near East," in G. E. Grunebaum & Roger Callois (eds.), The Dream and Human Societies. Berkeley: University of California Press, 1966

Kurt Seligman. Magic, Supernaturalism and Religion. New York: Random House, 1948, pp. 1–11.

Angus, Larry A. The Hidden Message of Jesus. Shelbyville, Kentucky: Wasteland Press, 2012.

Barrett, Sir William. Deathbed Visions. Guildfield, United Kingdom: White Crow Books, 2011.

Behe, Michael J. Darwin's Black Box. New York, NY: Free Press, 1996.

Brent, Bill J. Mind the Light. Brewster. Massachusetts: Paraclete Press, 2006.

Burns, David D. The Feeling Good Handbook. Ney York, NY: Plumb Printing, 1999.

Davidson, Gustav. A Dictionary of Angels: Including the Fallen Angels. New York, NY: The Free Press, 1971.

Ferrucci, Piero. Beauty and the Soul. New York, New York: Penguin Group, 2009.

Josef, Linda; Oates, Gary. "The Supernatural" The Ministry of Angels. Web 11/21/2013. http://sidroth.org/articles/ministry-angels.

Kempis, Thomas A. Imitation of Christ. Brewster, Massachusetts: Paraclete Press, 2008.

Kramarik, Akiane; Forelli Kramarik. Akiane: Her Life, Her art, Her Poetry. Nashville, Tennessee: w Publishing Group, 2006.

Kullman, Susan. "Intentional Wellness Coaching" Love Your Self. Web. 6 Sept. 2010. http://international wellness-coaching.com/blog/page/3/.

Lee, Desmond. PLATO The Republic. New York, New York: Penguin Books, 2001.

Moody, Raymond A, JR. LIFE AFTER LIFE. Simons Island, Georgia: Mockingbird Books, 1975.

Oats, Gary; Lamb, Robert Paul. Open My Life Lord. Moravian Falls, NC: Open Heaven Publications, 2004.

O'Donohue, John O. Divine Beauty. Great Britain: Bantam Press, 2003.

Phillips, Ron. Everyone's Guide to Demons. Lake Mary, Fl: Charisma House, 2010.

Piper, Don. 90 MINUTES IN HEAVEN. Grand Rapids, MI: Baker Publishing Group, 2004.

Richie, George. Return From Tomorrow. Grand Rapids, MI: Baker Publishing Group, 2007.

Rosenblum, Bruce; Kuttner, Fred. Quantum Enigma. Oxford, NY: Oxford University Press, 2011.

Storm, Howard. A Descent Into Hell: New York, New York: Doubleday Publishing, 2005.

Strong, James. Strong's Exhaustive Concordance of the Bible, Peabody, Ma. Hendrickson Publishers, 2009.

Thyer, Joseph H. Thyer's Greek-English Lexicon, New York: Harper & Brothers, 1889.

Waggoner, Robert. Lucid Dreaming. Neeham, Ma. Moment Point Press, 2008: Renew Books, 2011.

Wagner, Doris M. How to Cast Out Demons: A Guide to the Basics. Ventura, Ca: Renew Books, 2000.

Welton, Jonathan. The School of the Seers. Shippenburg, Pa. Destiny Image Publishers, Inc, 2013.

West, Fenny. "Inspiration4Generations" A Voice From Hell. Web 17 June 2011.

Williams, Kevin R. Nothing Better Than Death: Insights From 62 Profound Near-Death Experiences. Bloomington, Indiana: Xlibris, 2002.